THE BLESSED HOPE
CATECHISM

THE BLESSED HOPE
CATECHISM

ENTRUSTING THE GOSPEL TO THE NEXT GENERATION

ADVENT CHRISTIAN
GENERAL CONFERENCE

Xulon Press

Xulon Press
2301 Lucien Way #415
Maitland, FL 32751
407.339.4217
www.xulonpress.com

© 2018 by Advent Christian General Conference

All rights reserved solely by the author. The author guarantees all contents are original and do not infringe upon the legal rights of any other person or work. No part of this book may be reproduced in any form without the permission of the author. The views expressed in this book are not necessarily those of the publisher.

Unless otherwise indicated, Scripture quotations taken from the English Standard Version (ESV). Copyright © 2001 by Crossway, a publishing ministry of Good News Publishers. Used by permission. All rights reserved.

Printed in the United States of America.

ISBN-13: 9781545644256

TABLE OF CONTENTS

Preface xi
Introduction... xiii

PART 1 – FOUNDATIONS
What Is a Catechism? 1
What Is the Gospel? 7
Summary Statement 11

PART 2 - CATECHISM
Section 1: God 15
Summary
Questions 1-15

Section 2: Creation.. 25
Summary
Questions 16-29

Section 3: Sin 35
Summary
Questions 30-48

Section 4: Savior and Salvation.............................46
Summary
Questions 49-72

Section 5: Christ and Covenant.............................60
Summary
Questions 73-88

Section 6: Spirit, Sanctification and Scripture................71
Summary
Questions 89-110

Section 7: Community and Kingdom Living..................84
Summary
Questions 111-136

Section 8: Resurrection.....................................100
Summary
Questions 137-146

Section 9: New Heaven and New Earth.....................109
Summary
Questions 147-160

PART 3 - USING THE CATECHISM IN THE FAMILY
A Suggested Plan for Families 119
Helpful Resources 126

Table Of Contents

PART 4 - USING THE CATECHISM IN THE FAMILY OF GOD
Suggestions for Churches...................................*127*

PART 5 - ADDITIONAL RESOURCES
Annotated Glossary..*131*
Topical Index..*153*
Declaration of Principles *155*
Advent Christian Statement of Faith *159*

Preface

This book has been prepared by a small team of pastors and scholars who examined the original Advent Christian Catechism and its various editions, consulted other great catechisms both ancient (e.g., Augustine's Enchiridion on Faith, Hope, and Love), aged (the Westminster Catechism, the Heidelberg Catechism, both Luther and Calvin's catechisms, The Children's Catechism) and modern (John Piper's Baptist Catechism, Timothy Keller's New City Catechism) for comparative analysis, and dug deep into Holy Scripture to pan for its most basic grains of gold that would be essential and foundational for Christian growth and maturity within the family and the church. After more than three years, we are proud to present something that can be adapted for kids in kindergarten, high school students and adults, for individuals and families, and for training towards church membership and baptism.

While many will contend that only Bible stories or the Bible directly is needed for such instruction, this catechism is based precisely upon the Bible (and the accompanying curriculum illustrates each question with Bible stories), yet at the same time pulls out propositional statements that bring clarity to young minds. Each succinct statement is a pillar helping to connect us on the ground to the full weight of God's Word above. The goal is not simply data, or information or knowledge, but the application of God's truth - incarnate wisdom, we might say, that gives birth to new desires for God in all his transcendent beauty. Someone once said, "We become what we love and who we love shapes what we become." We want all who study this catechism to love God and be shaped by his Spirit into the image of his glorious Son.

A basic tenet of gardening is that the roots go as deep as the water flows, and so shallow watering produces shallow roots, and deep watering forms deep roots. It is our heartfelt prayer that this catechism be a well-needed rainstorm during these times of spiritual drought.

All Bible verses are from the English Standard Version. However, churches and families are encouraged to look them up in the translation they find most helpful for the purpose of Bible memory.

Soli Deo Gloria,
Michael Alix, MDiv
Nicholas Foss, MDiv
Matthew W. Larkin, MRE
Corey J. McLaughlin, MANT, MATH
Andrew J. Rice, MANT, MATH

Introduction

> Jesus is coming, tell the glad story;
> Ring out the message, swell the refrain;
> Coming with angels, coming in glory;
> Coming on earth forever to reign ...
> - George W. Sederquist, "Jesus Is Coming"

These lyrics by George W. Sederquist accurately capture the rallying cry of Advent Christians for more than a century-and-a-half. From their pulpits, in their publications, at their camp meetings and prophecy conferences, and in their hymns, Advent Christians have proclaimed this blessed hope: the soon return of Jesus Christ.

This *Blessed Hope Catechism* fully embraces the Advent Christian tradition and truly seeks to "tell the glad story" to the coming generations. To that end, the melody has changed, but the message is the same. The primary thread that runs through the catechism is the glorious hope that belongs to all who trust in Christ. As we eagerly await the new heaven and new earth, we desire to tell the old, old story in a fresh and engaging way, so that all who come behind us might know the Lord and the wonders he has done.

In its breadth, this new catechism is comprehensive, covering the major categories of Christian doctrine with sufficient balance for each. In its depth, we have sought clarity without compromise in theological precision. Most importantly, in its theology, we have pursued a Christ-centered approach, so that all who study this catechism might come to know Christ as the all-sufficient Savior who is before all things and in whom all things hold together.

The opening and closing questions serve as bookends to the doctrine in between. From the very beginning, the aim of this catechism is to open our eyes to the amazing hope and soul-satisfying joy that is ours through Jesus Christ, which will be made complete in the new heaven and new earth. Throughout the catechism, we turn our attention to the intersection of doctrine and life, seeking to wed the truth of our blessed hope with the reality of our everyday lives.

If this catechism does anything to ground us in the trustworthiness of Scripture, to inspire awe in the greatness and glory of God, to cause us to marvel at his truly amazing and sovereign grace, and to fully embrace the hope offered through the gospel of Jesus Christ - a hope that transcends the many trials and tribulations of this life - then it will have fulfilled its purpose.

Surely this catechism can be used to know more about God, but the greater reward - indeed, our greatest satisfaction in this

Introduction

life and the life to come - is to be known by God. As Sederquist's famed hymn says later on, he is

> Hope of the ages, and joy of the faithful,
> Long by the prophets of Israel foretold,
> Regal in splendor, transcendent in beauty,
> King of the saints, and Judge of the world.

May each one who reads and studies this catechism come to know this hope and this King.

PART 1 - FOUNDATIONS
What Is a Catechism?

When Luke, the well-known disciple of the apostle Paul and a doctor turned missionary, sat down to pen the longest contribution to the New Testament, he reminded Theophilus that he had previously been "instructed" in the Word (Luke 1:4). Apollos too, we are told, was also "instructed in the way of the Lord" (Acts 18:25). The Greek word in both cases is *katecheo*, which we derive our English word "catechism" from. *Katecheo* literally means "to sound down," as a teacher standing over a student might do as they verbally teach him or her. Thus, it was a form of oral instruction likely based on a similar rabbinic practice of asking questions and probing for answers. This is the very thing we see Jesus doing as a young boy in the temple and being done to him (Luke 2:46-47) and contributed to his "growing in wisdom and stature."

Since the earliest Christians were Jews who met in synagogues and on the temple grounds, it would make sense if they borrowed from their Jewish heritage to immediately begin training their children in the truth of Jesus Christ and his teaching using a similar method.

The goal of *katecheo* is multigenerational faith (Deut. 4:9; 6; Ex. 10:2): living faith that is passed on from one generation to another (e.g., Ps. 78:4-6). Already in the nascent church we see deep roots of doctrine plunging beneath the surface and the vibrant fruit of faith blossoming above. A faithful woman, Lois, teaches her daughter Eunice the way of faith. Her daughter grows up and teaches her son, Timothy, that same faith and zeal, and he grows up to be discipled by the apostle Paul (2 Tim. 1:5).

What exactly *katecheo* looked like for Timothy we cannot say, but we do know his mother read him the Scriptures and began his training even while he was just an infant (2 Tim. 3:15). We also know that it was Paul's customary method to teach via discussion. The word typically rendered "he reasoned with" is *dialegomai,* more accurately understood as a "dialogue with" others, a conversation, a give-and-take, a type of free-flowing question-and-answer (Acts 17:2, 17; 18:4; 19:8-9; 20:7). This is seen to some extent in Deuteronomy when God tells what the children will ask (6:20) and then tells the parents how to answer (vv. 21-25; also Josh. 4:21-24), expecting them to teach their children and their children's children the fear of the Lord (Deut. 6:2).

In this sense, God provides not only the content of the biblical questions through his Word, but lays down a basic methodology for how to teach the next generation as well:

Deut. 6:4-9: *"Hear, O Israel: The L*ORD *our God, the L*ORD *is one. You shall love the L*ORD *your God with all your heart and with all your soul and with all your might. And these words that I command you today shall be on your heart. You shall teach them diligently to your children, and shall talk of them when you sit in your house, and when you walk by the way, and when you lie down, and when you rise. You shall bind them as a sign on your hand, and they shall be as frontlets between your eyes. You shall write them on the doorposts of your house and on your gates. ..."*

The Hebrew word "to teach" (*shanan*) means to sharpen and is used to describe sharpened arrows that pierce the armor of the enemy (Isa. 5:28; Ps. 45:5). This was far more than teaching children stories; it involved teaching meaning, doctrine, theology and truth. This was no mere solitary Sunday school lesson, but an ongoing conversation for the Hebrew children as they stacked wood, picked figs, sat to play or lay down to sleep. If the Word of God is a sword, then this is far more than placing it in the hands of children, it is teaching them how to wield it in battle for their defense and protection (Eph. 6:17; Heb. 4:12).

God not only provides the content and the methodology, but also the primary context for this training (i.e. the family). Notice how Moses moves easily from speaking to the nation in

Deuteronomy 6:1 to the entire family (vv. 2-9), society's most basic unit. This privilege is granted to both parents as well:

> **Prov. 1:8-9:** *Hear, my son, your father's instruction, and forsake not your mother's teaching, for they are a graceful garland for your head and pendants for your neck.*

> **Prov. 6:20:** *My son, keep your father's commandment, and forsake not your mother's teaching.*

Such admonition is repeated throughout Proverbs (e.g., 3:1-3; 4:1-13, 20-23; 23:22, 26) and also characterizes the virtuous mother of Proverbs 31 who "opens her mouth with wisdom, and the teaching of kindness [to her family] is on her tongue" (v. 26).

In the New Testament, the apostle Paul charges the head of the family in particular (though, as we have seen, both parents are integral to the process):

> **Eph. 6:4:** *Fathers, do not provoke your children to anger, but bring them up in the discipline and instruction of the Lord.*

The first word translated discipline or training is *paideia*. In English, we get our words "pedagogy" and "pedagogical" from this word, which gives it an educational overtone and places the emphasis on scholastic training. In the Greek, it carries different connotations, namely, moral training; a training in righteousness accomplished by using the Scriptures (2 Tim. 3:16). It also carries the idea of receiving discipline for things that are morally wrong (Heb. 12:5, 7-8, 11). Thus, parents are to train their children in moral education and moral wisdom before God.

The second word translated "instruction" is *nouthesia*, which primarily carries the meaning of admonishment or warning for displeasing the Lord. Thus, Paul tells of the Old Testament saints who did not please the Lord (1 Cor. 10:5), of whom 23,000 were slain for their sexual immorality (vv. 6-8) and others destroyed for putting Christ to the test and grumbling (vv. 9-10). This story reminds the Corinthians that all the stories in the Old Testament are written down "for our instruction" (v. 11). Here "instruction" most certainly means "warning."

Thus, parents are to train their children in righteousness, correcting spiritual disorder, disciplining moral negligence and warning their children of the destructive consequences of following their sin.

Throughout Scripture, the family is seen as the linchpin of society and the keystone of culture, that which held the nation together and protected it against the pagan onslaught of the godless heathen (Deut. 4:9; 11:19; 29:29; 32:46; Ps. 78:3-8). Therefore, any biblical vision for educating our children within the church must not seek to supplant the authority of the family, or take away their special onus of responsibility, but must instead seek to supplement it with robust pillars of faith.

Does this catechism do all of this? Of course not, no one resource can. However, it does use God's content in a way that honors his revealed question-answer methodology, illustrates those questions and answers with biblical stories of both encouragement and warning, and places a spiritual pressure on parents within the church to be accountable to making sure they are activating their children's faith at home. In this sense, while the question-answer format of the catechism is not the *only* way to build on the bedrock of Christ, it is a formidable ally to help churches and parents fight for and claim the Promised Land inheritance of their child's heart.

Recommended Resources:

- Packer, J.I., and Gary Parrett. *Grounded in the Gospel: Building Believers the Old-Fashioned Way.*
- Parrett, Gary, and Steve Kang. *Teaching the Faith, Forming the Faithful: A Biblical Vision for Education in the Church.*

What Is the Gospel?

The fundamental purpose of this catechism is to hand down the truths of the Christian faith to another generation. In Psalm 78, Asaph writes, "We will not hide them from their children, but tell to the coming generation the glorious deeds of the LORD, and his might, and the wonders that he has done" (v. 4). Of all the wonders God has done, of all the glorious deeds of the Lord we are called to proclaim to the coming generations, the gospel of Jesus Christ is the most important.

The word "gospel" is the translation of the Greek word *euangelion*, which basically means "good news." In the New Testament, the word often occurs in a verbal form, *euangelizo* (from which we derive the word "evangelize"), and means "to proclaim or announce good news." The gospel of Jesus Christ, therefore, is the joyful announcement that forms the very heart of the Christian faith. By definition, the gospel is "news," not advice. It is not the announcement of what a person must *do*; rather, it is an announcement of what has *already been done*. Specifically, it is the announcement of what God has already done through

Jesus Christ, his Son, to bring about salvation and to usher in his kingdom.

So, what is the gospel? What is the good news of Christianity, the joyful proclamation of victory? One helpful way to summarize the gospel is using four simple words: God, Man, Christ, Response.

GOD

> There is one true God - Father, Son and Holy Spirit (Q. 2) - who is defined by his perfect holiness (Q. 9), that is, set apart from his creation, pure and without sin (Q. 10). God created the world and everything in it, including humanity (Qs. 16-17), in order that he might be glorified and that we might find our supreme joy in him (Q. 18).

MAN

> When God created Adam and Eve, our first parents (Q. 22), he made them holy and happy (Q. 23), but they chose to disobey God (Q. 31) and thus sin entered the world. Sin is the worship of anything other than God (Q. 32), which results in rejecting God's rule, ignoring his will, or disobeying his law (Q. 33). Because Adam was the representative for all humanity (Q. 38), we are all born guilty before God and with a sinful nature (Q. 41), thus we deserve the wrath and curse of God (Q. 47). Our sin has separated us from the

life of God (Q. 48). But, thanks be to God, he did not leave all humanity under his wrath and the curse of sin, but instead provided a way of salvation (Q. 49)!

CHRIST

The way of salvation provided by God was his Son, Jesus Christ, sent into the world to save all who believe (Q. 50). Jesus Christ, fully God and fully man (Q. 52), lived a perfect life of obedience, service and suffering (Q. 54). He became a substitute for sinners by his painful and shameful death on the cross, and thus satisfied the wrath of God toward sin (Qs. 55-56). Jesus not only died and was buried, but was raised to life on the third day and now reigns triumphantly at the right hand of the Father (Qs. 57-58). Because of his life, death and resurrection, we can now be declared innocent on the basis of Jesus' perfect righteousness (Q. 61), so that we are no longer God's enemies, but his friends (Q. 62).

RESPONSE

In order to experience this great gift of salvation, we must repent of our sin and believe this good news of Jesus Christ - his life, death, resurrection - and his coming kingdom (Qs. 63, 66). Repentance means that we are sorry for our sin, that we hate it and turn away from it by turning to God (Q. 64). Believing in the gospel means trusting fully in the finished work of Jesus Christ and loving him as Savior and Lord (Q. 68). When we repent of our sin and believe the gospel, we are welcomed into his family, the church (Q. 113), and given the hope of life and immortality with Christ forever in the new heaven and new earth (Qs. 144-145).

This is the glorious gospel of Jesus Christ and of his coming kingdom. What a joy it is to know, believe and proclaim this truth to the next generation.

> "We will not hide them from their children,
> but tell to the coming generation
> the glorious deeds of the Lord, and his might,
> and the wonders that he has done.
>
> ... that the next generation might know them,
> the children yet unborn,
> and arise and tell them to their children,
> so that they should set their hope in God ..."
> (Ps. 78:4-7)

Summary Statement

God the Father

We believe in God the Father Almighty, infinite and eternal in wisdom, love and power; Creator, Ruler, Sustainer and Restorer of all things.

God the Son

We believe in God the Son, the only Son, Jesus Christ, our Lord, fully divine and fully human, who was born of the Virgin Mary; who lived a sinless life; who accomplished our redemption through his substitutionary death on the cross; who secured our justification by his bodily resurrection from the dead; who ascended to the right hand of the Father, where he intercedes for us as our High Priest and Mediator; and who will return in power and glory to judge the living and the dead, and to reign eternally as King.

God the Holy Spirit

We believe in God the Holy Spirit, who proceeds from the Father and the Son; he was sent to convict the world of sin, of righteousness and of judgment; and to regenerate the hearts of sinful human beings, indwelling, sanctifying and sealing them until the day of redemption.

God Three in One

We believe that there is one God, eternally existing in three persons: Father, Son and Holy Spirit, who are co-equal in deity and united in holiness, having the same attributes and perfection.

Sin

We believe that mankind was created in the image of God with the potential for immortality, but that through Adam's sin came spiritual and physical death, alienating all of humanity from the life of God, thus forfeiting our immortality, whereby we now inherit our sinful nature, making it impossible to save ourselves.

Salvation

We believe that God grants salvation from his wrath and the curse of sin, and gives life and immortality in the age to come on the basis of the sinless life, substitutionary death and resurrection of Jesus Christ; by grace alone, through faith alone, to all those who repent of their sin and trust in Jesus Christ as Lord and Savior.

Scripture

We believe the original autographs of the Bible to be the verbally inspired, inerrant and authoritative Word of God, the only infallible standard of faith and practice.

Church

We believe that the church is created for the glory of God, committed to the mission of God to make disciples of all nations, united under the Lordship of Christ, comprised of all who confess Jesus as Lord and Savior and are born of the Spirit, and gathered on earth in local, ordered assemblies, which are called together to worship God, proclaim the gospel, celebrate the ordinances of believer's baptism and the Lord's Supper, while living as citizens of the kingdom of God as we eagerly await our blessed hope: the soon-coming return of Christ.

Resurrection

We believe in the personal, visible and imminent second coming of Jesus Christ to the earth for the establishment of his kingdom, and in the bodily resurrection of both the saved and the lost; they that are saved unto the resurrection of life and immortality, and they that are lost unto the resurrection of damnation and everlasting destruction.

New Heaven and New Earth

>We believe that the blessed hope of the believer is to live eternally in the presence of the triune God in the new heaven and new earth, his redeemed creation restored to its original perfection, raised to new life with new bodies, where we will be fully and forever free from sin and death, to live exclusively under the control of his Spirit in the righteousness of Christ for the glory of God the Father. Therefore, we believe this essential truth is an incentive for holy living and faithful proclamation of the gospel.

PART 2 - CATECHISM
Section 1: God

Summary

The study of God is the study of theology (*theos,* "God" and *logia,* "the study of"). Both in the world and in the church, the concept of God is often misunderstood, twisted or reformulated to fit modernist ears. Is he a "God of love" who never disciplines his children nor punishes the wicked? Is he merely a "God of vengeance," so blinded by rage and righteous indignation that all hope is lost? Is he the gift-giving "Santa Claus God" of the health and wealth movement who promises every financial blessing under heaven and the longevity to enjoy it? Which God is he and how is any ordinary person to know for certain?

Classic theology answers these questions by distinguishing between God's general and special revelation. His general revelation is manifest through creation, where his invisible attributes are seen (Rom. 1:18-23), as well as the conscience (Rom. 2:14-16) which, though evil because of the fall (Heb. 10:22; 1

Tim. 4:2), nonetheless reflects God's image (however distorted). These two together are enough information to reasonably conclude that a supreme being exists, that he is all powerful and that he desires some kind of a relationship (otherwise why create in the first place?). However, it is not enough to adequately identify this Being. That is why God made himself known in a special way through his consecrated Word, infallible and inerrant in all it intends to teach, and through Christ, the perfect, sinless, Son of God.

Thus, we learn through the consecrated, written Word and Christ, the perfect divine Word (John 1:1), that the greatest joy in this world and the next is to know and be known by God (Q. 1; John 17:3).

We also learn that this everlasting God is far more complex than we could have ever imagined; one God eternally existing (Q. 8) in three persons: Father, Son and Holy Spirit (Qs. 2, 6). While modern illustrations attempt to capture this Orthodox teaching (e.g., an egg has three parts, water has three states) they all fail to adequately portray the true mystery. In the end analysis, God is transcendent, therefore some of his qualities are simply unknowable (Isa. 55:8-9), and the depths of the riches of his nature are unfathomable.

The Father of creation reveals himself to us by his personal name Yahweh, the great I AM (Q. 3). Jesus is his Son, the promised anointed Messiah, our Lord and Savior (Q. 4). The Holy Spirit is no mere force as many believe, but the third person of the Godhead (Q. 5) who proceeds from the Father (John 14:26) and the Son (John 15:26), thus he is referred to at times as the "Spirit of the Father" (Matt. 10:20; Rom. 8:10-11; 2 Cor. 1:21-22; Eph. 3:14-16) and as the "Spirit of the Son" (Rom. 8:9; Gal. 4:6; Phil. 1:19; 1 Peter 1:11). He is described using masculine pronouns (i.e., "he" in John 15:26; 16:13-14) and presented as one who can be grieved (Eph. 4:30), sinned against (Isa. 63:10) and lied to (Acts 5:3). He is called our Helper and Counselor, and sent into God's people as a down payment of his intentions to return and redeem those upon whom his favor rests.

Strictly speaking, God is a spirit and therefore without corporeal existence (Q. 7). Jesus, however, took on humanity and will continue to exist in that state forever (John 1:14; Phil. 2:5-8).

God can be described theologically by his attributes, of which there are many; some he alone possesses and some he shares with humanity (Q. 11; see *attributes* in glossary as well). However, only once in Scripture is God ever announced to be supremely one thing above all other attributes. When Isaiah is raptured into the throne room of God, he hears the angels sing, "Holy, holy, holy" (Isa. 6:3). In Hebrew, a common way to express something as superlative is to repeat it three times. Therefore, the central hub of the wheel that holds all the other spokes together is the holiness of God.

While it is easy to get lost in the details of who God is, the fundamental point we want to live out and teach to others is that, beyond comprehension, this cosmic God who created everything longs to share himself with us so that he might be the object of our highest affection (Ps. 16:11; 37:4; Mark 12:30; Ex. 34:14) and we might be the object of his deepest delight (Ps. 147:11; 149:4; Zeph. 3:17). Getting God right puts everything else in proper perspective, but getting him wrong causes untold chaos and disorder. Our true identity, our peace, our stability in this tumultuous world, is all wrapped up with how we define and understand the God of the Bible. As deep calls out to deep, so God is calling you into the deep waters of his love. May you begin the journey anew.

Recommended Resources:
Please note that all recommended resources are listed with resources of easier readability at the top and more theological works at the bottom.

- Sproul, R.C. *The Holiness of God.*
- Ware, Bruce A. *Father, Son, and Holy Spirit: Relationships, Roles, and Relevance.*
- Snyder, John. *Behold Your God: Rethinking God Biblically* DVD. *beholdyourgod.org.*
- Tozer, A.W. *The Knowledge of the Holy.*
- Tozer, A.W. *The Pursuit of God.*
- Piper, John. *Desiring God: Meditations of a Christian Hedonist.*
- Packer, J.I. *Knowing God.*

GOD

1. **What is your supreme satisfaction in this age and the age to come?**
   To know and be known by God now and forevermore in the new heaven and the new earth.

   John 17:3: *And this is eternal life, that they know you, the only true God, and Jesus Christ whom you have sent.*

   See also Ps. 73:24-28; Jer. 9:23-24; 1 Cor. 8:3; Gal. 4:9; Phil. 3:10.

2. **Who is the one true God?**
   The Father, the Son and the Holy Spirit.

   Matt. 28:19: *"... Go therefore and make disciples of all nations, baptizing them in the name of the Father and of the Son and of the Holy Spirit, ..."*

   See also 2 Cor. 13:14; 1 John 5:7; 1 Peter 1:1-2; Rom. 14:17-18; 15:16; 1 Cor. 2:2-5; 6:11; 12:4-6; 2 Cor. 1:21-22; Gal. 4:6; Eph. 2:18-22; 3:14-19; 4:4-6; Col. 1:6-8; 1 Thess. 1:3-5; 2 Thess. 2:13-14; Titus 3:4-6.

3. **Who is God the Father?**

   He is Yahweh; the Creator, Ruler, Sustainer and Restorer of all things.

   Ex. 3:14: *God said to Moses, "I AM WHO I AM." And he said, "Say this to the people of Israel, 'I AM has sent me to you.'"*

   See also Gen. 1:1; Job 38:33-37; Ps. 135:6-7; 115:3; Isa. 40:23; Acts 17:28; Rev. 21:5-7; John 5:17.

4. **Who is God the Son?**

   He is Jesus, the Messiah, my Lord and Savior.

   Matt. 16:16: *Simon Peter replied, "You are the Christ, the Son of the living God."*

   See also Matt. 1:1; 3:17; John 20:28; 2 Peter 3:18.

5. **Who is God the Holy Spirit?**

   He is my Counselor, Comforter and Teacher.

   John 14:16-17: *"... And I will ask the Father, and he will give you another Helper, to be with you forever, even the Spirit of truth, whom the world cannot receive, because it neither sees him nor* *knows him. You know him, for he dwells with you and will be in you. ..."*

See also John 14:26; 15:26; 16:13; 2 Tim. 1:14.

6. Is there more than one true God?

No. There is only one true God who eternally exists in three persons.

Deut. 6:4: *"Hear, O Israel: The LORD our God, the LORD is one. ..."*

See also Isa. 45:5; 1 Cor. 8:4-6; Jer. 10:10.

7. What is God?

God is a spirit and does not have a body like men.

John 4:24: *"... God is spirit, and those who worship him must worship in spirit and truth."*

See also John 1:18; Col. 1:15.

8. Who made God?

No one made God; He is from everlasting to everlasting.

Gen. 1:1-2: *In the beginning, God created the heavens and the earth. The earth was without form and void, and darkness was over the face of the deep. And the Spirit of God was hovering over the face of the waters.*

See also Ps. 90:2; Rom. 1:20.

9. **What is the defining attribute of God?**
God is holy, holy, holy.

Isa. 6:3: *And one called to another and said: "Holy, holy, holy is the LORD of hosts; the whole earth is full of his glory!"*

See also Isa. 6:4-8; 1 Peter 1:16; Rev. 4:8.

10. **What does it mean that God is holy?**
He is set apart from his creation, pure and without sin.

Ex. 15:11: *"Who is like you, O LORD, among the gods? Who is like you, majestic in holiness, awesome in glorious deeds, doing wonders? ..."*

See also Ex. 3:5-6; Lev. 20:6; 1 Sam. 2:2; Ps. 5:4; Isa. 59:2; 1 John 1:5; Rev. 15:4;

11. What are some other attributes of God?

He is infinite, eternal and unchanging with wisdom, love, power and truth.

See Ex. 3:14; 34:6-7; Job 11:7-9; 42:2; 1 Tim. 6:15-16; Rom. 16:27; Deut. 32:4; Jer. 32:17; Ps. 86:11; 1 John 4:8,16; James 1:17.

12. Where is God?

He is everywhere.

Ps. 139:7: *Where shall I go from your Spirit? Or where shall I flee from your presence?*

See also Ps. 139:1-13; 46:1; Isa. 57:15; Prov. 15:3.

13. Does God know all things?

Yes. Nothing can be hidden from God.

1 John 3:20: *[F]or whenever our heart condemns us, God is greater than our heart, and he knows everything.*

See also Ps. 139:4; Isa. 46:9-10; Heb. 4:13.

14. Can God do all things?

Yes. God can do all his holy will.

Job 42:2: *"I know that you can do all things, and that no purpose of yours can be thwarted. ..."*

See also Gen. 18:14; Num. 11:23; Jer. 32:17; Mark 14:36.

15. Is God in complete control of all things at all times?
Yes. He works all things for the good of those who love him.

Rom. 8:28: *And we know that for those who love God all things work together for good, for those who are called according to his purpose.*

See also Gen. 50:20; 2 Chron. 20:6; Ps. 115:3; Isa. 45:6-7; 55:8-11; Heb. 1:3.

Section 2: Creation

Summary

What we think about ourselves affects not only our identity, but also our general behavior and the specific choices we make. If someone believes human origins are explained in the theory of atheistic evolution and common descent from a shared ancestor of the chimpanzees, then they will inevitably view themselves as animals as well. The foundation for morality soon becomes quicksand rather than bedrock. It is vital that we know who we are, where we came from, the value we have and the hope we hold onto for full redemption.

In one sense, it is absolutely basic for the Christian to ask, "Who made me?" and to answer, "God did" (Q. 16). Yet, when Genesis is compared to other ancient stories of its era (e.g., the Babylonian myths), we discover that the pagan gods formed all things from a pre-existing substance, not like the God of the Bible who created out of nothing.

These pagan deities also formed humanity for a specific purpose: to be their slaves, to do their labor for them and to be in subjugation to them. The God of the Bible stands in stark contrast, creating humanity instead as the high point of his divine work and taking pleasure in us in order that we take pleasure in him (Q. 18).

Genesis chapter one portrays God as the Almighty Creator of all things who acts with absolute authority and endless power do all his holy will. Creation itself reflects the very attributes of God and therefore reveals both something of his nature and his character (Q. 20; Rom. 1:20).

Chapter two of Genesis reveals a new name for the Almighty Creator: Yahweh - the personal name of God first revealed to Moses at the burning bush. It is true that he could have fashioned humanity after anything he had already made; instead, Yahweh intimately and personally formed humanity after his very own image, both male and female (Q. 21). God's image can be seen in the union of marriage when both are joined together as one, and in humanity's ability to reason, think and create, on a higher level than animals. Any similarity between humans and animals, then, is understood by Christians not as evidence of common descent, but rather as evidence of a common designer.

Perhaps most of all, being made in God's image means being given God's authority to rule as his representatives on earth (Q. 25; Gen. 1:28). Though marred in the fall, this privilege will be regained when Christians reign with Christ on his throne at his return (2 Tim. 2:11-13; Rev. 2:26; 5:10; 20:6), even one day judging angels (1 Cor. 6:3).

When God imprinted his image on Adam and Eve, he placed eternity in their hearts that they might seek for, long after and pursue him (Eccl. 3:11). They were sinless and innocent, though not perfect. If they were perfect, they would be unable to sin at all. Instead, Adam and Eve stood on spiritually neutral ground able to sin or not sin according to their own free will. But after the fall, all humanity became corrupted and ravished by sin that polluted every part of their minds, their wills and their emotions, leaving humankind unable to do anything but sin (Jer. 17:9; Mark 7:21-23; Rom. 5:6; Eph. 2:1-3). While we can do much that appears "good" by our human standard, God's standard is perfection (Matt. 5:48), so he can say "there is none who does good, not even one" (Ps. 14:3). Christ redeems us and gives us his Spirit in this realm to fight sin (Gal. 5:17), but one day, he will make his holy ones unable to sin at all in his kingdom (1 John 3:2).

Adam and Eve were created as mature teenagers, perhaps, or adults, and placed in God's garden paradise under God's watchful eye and tender care (Q. 26). Though God alone possesses innate immortality as part of his nature (Q. 24), Adam and Eve were created with the potential for immortality; ageless living and never-ending life could have been theirs. Remember, two important trees stood in the garden of Eden: the Tree of the Knowledge of Good and Evil and the Tree of Life (Q. 27). One tree was to test their obedience (Q. 29) and the other to reward their faithfulness if they obeyed (Q. 28).

It is sometimes wrongly assumed that God took away the reward of immortality as a punishment for their sins. However, a careful reading of Genesis chapter three tells us a different story. God punishes the serpent (vv. 14-15) and pronounces the effect of the curse of sin upon the woman (v. 16) and the man (vv. 17-19). The choice to rebel against God will now be a first impulse of every child they have from the womb onward (Ps. 51:5). God's concern is that they may reach out and eat from the Tree of Life and live forever. So, he drives them out. Here we actually see a Father's love. In Genesis 3, he immediately announces a plan to send someone who might battle Satan and win (v. 15). Then he graciously clothes his rebellious children with garments to cover their nakedness (v. 21) and, finally, prohibits them from making their situation irrevocably disastrous by eating of the Tree of Life and living in eternal sinful corruption. Their banishment was more about protecting them than about punishing them. One day, he will call them back and grant them the right to eat from the Tree of Life (Rev. 2:7) that will be planted in the New Jerusalem, the paradise of God (22:2).

Until that day, even creation "waits with eager longing for the revealing of the sons of God" (Rom. 8:19). Unlike the world that cannot distinguish between the Creator and his creation and those in the world who worship all aspects of nature, Christians are called to creation-care and stewardship of the earth (Q. 25) until it is finally "set free from its bondage to corruption" and we "obtain the freedom of the glory of the children of God" (v. 21).

Recommended Resources:

- Lifeway Adults. *The Gospel Project: God the Creator* (Bible Study Series).
- Tozer, A.W. *Delighting in God.*
- Strobel, Lee. *The Case for a Creator.*
- Calvin, John. *God the Creator.*

CREATION

16. Who made you?
God made me.

Gen. 1:27: *So God created man in his own image, in the image of God he created him; male and female he created them.*

See also Ps. 139:14.

17. What else did God make?
God made all things.

Col. 1:16: *For by him all things were created, in heaven and on earth, visible and invisible, whether thrones or dominions or rulers or authorities - all things were created through him and for him.*

See also Gen. 1:1; Acts 4:24; Eph. 3:9; Rev. 4:11.

18. Why did God make you and all things?
For his own glory and good pleasure, and our supreme joy in him.

Rev. 4:11: *"Worthy are you, our Lord and God, to receive glory and honor and power, for you created* *all things, and by your will they existed and were created."*

See also Ps. 16:11; 37:4; 149:4; Col. 1:16.

19. How did God create all things?

He created all things out of nothing by his Word.

Heb. 11:3: *By faith we understand that the universe was created by the word of God, so that what is seen was not made out of things that are visible.*

See also John 1:1-4; Col. 1:16.

20. What does creation tell us about God?

Creation reflects his beauty and majesty.

Ps. 19:1: *The heavens declare the glory of God, and the sky above proclaims his handiwork.*

See also Ps. 8:1; Rom. 1:20.

21. How did God create humanity?

God created them, male and female in his image.

Gen. 1:27: *So God created man in his own image, in the image of God he created him; male and female he created them.*

See also Gen. 5:1.

22. Who were our first parents?
Adam and Eve.

Gen. 3:20: *The man called his wife's name Eve, because she was the mother of all living.*

23. In what condition did God make Adam and Eve?
He made them holy and happy.

Gen. 1:31: *And God saw everything that he had made, and behold, it was very good. And there was evening and there was morning, the sixth day.*

See also Rom. 5:12-13; 2 Cor. 3:18; Col. 3:9-10; Eph. 4:24.

24. Did God create Adam and Eve with immortality?
No, God alone has immortality.

1 Tim. 6:15-16: *... he who is the blessed and only Sovereign, the King of kings and Lord of lords, who alone has immortality, who dwells in unapproachable light, whom no one has ever seen or can see. To him be honor and eternal dominion. Amen.*

See also 1 Tim. 1:17; 2 Tim. 1:10; Rom. 2:7; Rev. 2:7.

25. What authority did God give Adam and Eve?

To rule over all of his creation.

Gen. 1:26: *Then God said, "Let us make man in our image, after our likeness. And let them have dominion over the fish of the sea and over the birds of the heavens and over the livestock and over all the earth and over every creeping thing that creeps on the earth."*

See also Gen. 1:28; 2:15.

26. Where did God place Adam and Eve?

In the garden of Eden.

Gen. 2:15: *The LORD God took the man and put him in the garden of Eden to work it and keep it.*

27. What did God place in the middle of Eden?

The Tree of Life and the Tree of the Knowledge of Good and Evil.

Gen. 2:9: *And out of the ground the LORD God made to spring up every tree that is pleasant to the sight and good for food. The tree of life was in* the midst of the garden, and the tree of the knowledge of good and evil.

28. Why did God create the Tree of Life?

To grant immortality to those who eat of it.

Gen. 3:22-23: *Then the LORD God said, "Behold, the man has become like one of us in knowing good and evil. Now, lest he reach out his hand and take also of the tree of life and eat, and live forever -" therefore the LORD God sent him out from the garden of Eden to work the ground from which he was taken.*

29. Why did God create the Tree of the Knowledge of Good and Evil?

To test Adam and Eve's obedience.

Gen. 2:17: *"... but of the tree of the knowledge of good and evil you shall not eat, for in the day that you eat of it you shall surely die."*

Section 3: Sin

Summary

What is sin? Plantinga, a Christian philosopher, summarizes it with two words: "lawlessness" and "faithlessness."

The technical name for the study of sin is *hamartiology*. It is made up of the two Greek words *hamartia* ("missing the mark") and *logia* ("the study of"). In its simplest form, then, sin is missing the mark of God's holy, perfect standard (Matt. 5:48). God created Adam and Eve to be in a relationship with him and gave them only one prohibition (Q. 30). Choosing to eat from the forbidden tree was not simply failure on their part, it was an act of rebellion against God - a sin to be sure (Q. 31), but more specifically, it was idolatry (Q. 32): namely, the worship of self in trying to be like God. In the same way that a few drops of poison in a drink spread to the whole, so this rebellious sin spread through all their being, affecting their mind, will and emotions (Q. 33).

Satan's temptation (Q. 34) also resulted in fear and shame of being in the presence of God (Q. 35; John 3:19-20). Ironically, had they remained faithful to God, he would have made Adam and Eve like him anyway (Q. 36), living forever in sinless, perfect unity. Instead, the corruption of sin spread further, affecting God's good creation itself (Q. 37) and penetrating to all the descendants of Adam and Eve (Q. 38), thus bringing suffering, sorrow, pain and death to all humanity (Q. 39). From this seed of original sin (Q. 40) grows the bad tree of the sinful nature in all mankind (Q. 41; Matt. 7:18-19) that then bears the bad fruit of making sinful choices, thinking sinful thoughts and feeling sinful feelings (Q. 42).

The universal pandemic of sin is found in all humans from birth (Ps. 51:5). In our pride, we may be tempted to think sin is merely a "mistake" or a few minor peccadilloes that we commit. So, God wrote his law on tablets of stone and upon the human heart to show us the severity of our sin (Q. 43). The hundreds of commands revealed in Holy Scripture (Q. 44) were never meant to be a ladder to earn one's way into heaven, but a mirror to show us our true filthiness before the throne (Q. 45). The absence of the written law of God in any given culture, however, does not make humanity any less culpable since the basics of his will are impressed upon their conscience (Q. 46). God has revealed himself through creation, the conscience and the consecrated Word so that all are without excuse when weighed in the scales of his justice (Q. 47).

What we discover when looking into the mirror of God's law is that, in our depravity, we are totally unable to produce any spiritual and lasting good (Rom. 3:10-18; Heb. 11:6). We constantly lean toward sin and lack any natural ability to change this into a love for God. We desperately need a savior to save us from ourselves.

Perhaps the worst and most heinous perversion of sin is that it distorts, destroys and separates humanity from life in God (Q. 48). In creation, God created all things with unity and peace to worship and glorify him, this is God's *shalom* (the Hebrew word translated "peace"). Sin disrupts God's shalom, but the Prince of Shalom who was promised back in Genesis, born of a virgin, raised from the dead and coming back in glory has already started restoring our life to him and will complete it when he returns (Phil. 1:6).

Recommended Resources for this Section:

- Bridges, Jerry. *Respectable Sins: Confronting the Sins We Tolerate.*
- Plantinga Jr., Cornelius. *Not the Way It's Supposed to Be: A Breviary of Sin.*
- Hoekema, Anthony. *Created in God's Image.*

SIN

30. What did God say to Adam and Eve when he placed them in the garden of Eden?

To eat of every tree in the garden except the Tree of the Knowledge of Good and Evil.

Gen. 2:16-17: *And the LORD God commanded the man, saying, "You may surely eat of every tree of the garden, but of the tree of the knowledge of good and evil you shall not eat, for in the day that you eat of it you shall surely die."*

31. What did Adam and Eve choose?

To sin by eating of the forbidden tree.

Gen. 3:6: *So when the woman saw that the tree was good for food, and that it was a delight to the eyes, and that the tree was to be desired to make one wise, she took of its fruit and ate, and she also gave some to her husband who was with her, and he ate.*

32. What is sin?

The worship of anything other than God, which is idolatry.

Rom. 1:25: ... *because they exchanged the truth about God for a lie and worshiped and served the creature rather than the Creator, who is blessed forever! Amen.*

See also Ex. 20:3; 34:14; Isa. 42:8; 44:12-17; Ezek. 14:3; Gal. 5:19-21; Col. 3:5.

33. What is the result of idolatry in the human heart?
Rejecting God's rule, ignoring his will and disobeying his law.

Rom. 3:10-12: *[A]s it is written: "None is righteous, no, not one; no one understands; no one seeks for God. All have turned aside; together they have become worthless; no one does good, not even one."*

See also Jer. 5:23; Isa. 53:6; Rom. 1:18; 3:23; 1 Cor. 6:9-10.

34. Who tempted Adam and Eve to sin?
Satan tempted Eve first and used her to tempt Adam.

Gen. 3:13: *Then the LORD God said to the woman, "What is this that you have done?" The woman said, "The serpent deceived me, and I ate."*

35. What happened to Adam and Eve when they disobeyed God?

They became afraid and ashamed and were no longer sinless.

Gen. 3:7: *Then the eyes of both were opened, and they knew that they were naked. And they sewed fig leaves together and made themselves loincloths.*

36. What inheritance was lost as a result of Adam's sin in the garden?

The privilege of eating from the Tree of Life and living forever with God.

Gen. 3:23-24: *[T]herefore the LORD God sent him out from the garden of Eden to work the ground from which he was taken. He drove out the man, and at the east of the garden of Eden he placed the cherubim and a flaming sword that turned every way to guard the way to the tree of life.*

37. What effect did Adam's sin have on God's good creation?

All creation is now corrupted and groaning for redemption.

Rom. 8:20-21: *For the creation was subjected to futility, not willingly, but because of him who subjected it, in hope that the creation itself will be set free from its bondage to corruption and obtain the freedom of the glory of the children of God.*

See also Gen. 3:17; Rom. 8:22.

38. Did Adam represent you in the garden?

Yes, me and all people.

1 Cor. 15:22: *For as in Adam all die, so also in Christ shall all be made alive.*

See also Rom. 5:12-21.

39. What effect did Adam's sin have on you and all people?

It brought suffering, sorrow, pain and death.

Rom. 5:12: *Therefore, just as sin came into the world through one man, and death through sin, and so death spread to all men because all sinned ...*

See also Rom. 6:23.

40. What do you now inherit from Adam?

Original sin.

Rom. 5:12: *Therefore, just as sin came into the world through one man, and death through sin, and so death spread to all men because all sinned ...*

See also Eph. 2:1-3.

41. What is the effect of original sin?

I am born guilty and with a sinful nature.

Ps. 51:5: *Behold, I was brought forth in iniquity, and in sin did my mother conceive me.*

See also Job 15:14-16; Ps. 14:2-3.

42. What is the effect of your sinful nature?

I now make sinful choices, think sinful thoughts and feel sinful feelings.

Rom. 7:18: *For I know that nothing good dwells in me, that is, in my flesh. For I have the desire to do what is right, but not the ability to carry it out.*

Section 3: Sin

See also Jer. 17:9; Isa. 53:6; Gal. 5:19-21.

43. How do you know that you are sinning?
God has given me his law in the Bible and on my heart.

Rom. 1:21: *For although they knew God, they did not honor him as God or give thanks to him, but they became futile in their thinking, and their foolish hearts were darkened.*

See also Rom. 1:20.

44. How has God given you his law in the Bible?
Through hundreds of commands, especially the Ten Commandments.

John 1:17: *For the law was given through Moses; grace and truth came through Jesus Christ.*

See also Deut. 6:17-18; Ex. 20:1-17; Neh. 10:29.

45. What is the purpose of the law?
To show that all fall short of God's perfect standard.

Rom. 7:7: *What then shall we say? That the law is sin? By no means! Yet if it had not been for the* *law, I would not have known sin. For I would not have known what it is to covet if the law had not said, "You shall not covet."*

See also Rom. 3:23; 5:20; 7:8-9; Matt. 5:17-48.

46. How has God written his law on your heart?
He has given me a conscience so that I feel shame and guilt when I sin.

Rom. 2:15: *They show that the work of the law is written on their hearts, while their conscience also bears witness, and their conflicting thoughts accuse or even excuse them …*

See also Isa. 30:21.

47. What does every sin deserve?
The wrath and curse of God.

Rom. 1:18: *For the wrath of God is revealed from heaven against all ungodliness and unrighteousness of men, who by their unrighteousness suppress the truth.*

See also Rom. 6:23; Eph. 2:3; Col. 3:6; 1 Thess. 1:10.

48. What does sin do to your relationship with God?
It separates me from the life of God.

Eph. 4:18: *They are darkened in their understanding, alienated from the life of God because of the ignorance that is in them, due to their hardness of heart.*

See also Isa. 59:2.

Section 4: Savior and Salvation

Summary

God has promised to deal with sin. In Eden, he promised death to those who violate his will and act in disobedience. So, those who sin stand justly condemned before God, deserving of death because "the soul who sins shall die" (Ezek. 18:20; also Rom. 6:23). It would then be right and fair for God to leave humanity to its own twisted devices; yet the same compassionate Father who protected Adam and Eve from doing more harm by driving them out of the garden, and protected them from the elements by making them cloths of animal skin, also provided the way of salvation for his elect (Q. 49). And who are his elect? All who receive him, who believe in his name; to them "he gave the right to become children of God" (John 1:12).

The Old Testament sacrificial system was God's way of balancing his justice (which demands death for sin) and his mercy (which requires not receiving the full penalty of his wrath). But the blood of bulls and goats was only a temporary solution;

something more was needed. *Someone* more was needed (Heb. 9:11-10:25). So, God sent his sinless Son to be the perfect once-and-for-all-time sacrifice (Q. 50).

To make possible man's redemption, God works through his Son, the Lord Jesus Christ, made in the likeness of humanity (Phil. 2:7; Heb. 2:14-18), to become both the sinner's substitute and his salvation. Jesus came into the world conceived by the Holy Spirit and born of the Virgin Mary (Q. 51). The One who is fully God emptied himself of his rights and privileges of God and became fully human (Phil. 2:5-7), two natures joined together for all time (Q. 52). This is the mystery of the incarnation: God became flesh and dwelt among us (John 1:14).

In the incarnation, however, Jesus was not marked or stained by original sin (Q. 53). Through this and the help of the Spirit of God, he lived a life of obedience, service and suffering (Q. 54). And because of his sinless life, Jesus could be our substitute by his death on the cross, our vicarious sin-bearer, our perfect sacrifice, and therefore satisfy the wrath of God for all who believe (Qs. 55-56). This propitiation for our sin (i.e., satisfaction of God's wrath) made possible not only the suspension of our penalty, but also undeserved forgiveness and justification in God's sight.

Three days after his death, Jesus rose bodily from the grave (Q. 57). This resurrection is the sign that Jesus' death perfectly atoned for our sin. His sacrifice was accepted by God. After this, he ascended bodily to the right hand of the Father (Q. 58). One day Jesus will return to earth in the same way that he ascended, in power and glory (Q. 59).

Through Jesus' resurrection from the dead, he secured justification for all who believe (Q. 60) and bear fruit in keeping with that profession (John 15:8) - that is, those who trust in Christ's substitutionary death and bodily resurrection are declared innocent based on his righteousness (Q. 61). The Lord Jesus became our victorious life-giver, defeating sin by his sinless death and death by his triumphant resurrection, delivering us from their stranglehold and unleashing a new Spirit of life within us. The Spirit not only makes possible our forgiveness and justification, but also our sanctification to holiness. Through all of this, we are no longer God's enemies, but his friends (Q. 62).

Having considered the wonder of God's salvation, we are left with one lingering question: What must we do to be saved? We must repent of our sins and believe the gospel of Jesus Christ (Q. 63). The word "repent" literally means "to change one's mind." Thus, we change our mind about who Christ is, from a mere man to the God-man, and we change our mind about sin from something that is acceptable to something that is offensive to God. The idea of repentance is both a turning away from something (sin) for which we now regret and hate and a turning to something (God's grace in Christ) for which we desire (Qs. 64-65).

In order for someone to turn from his sin and turn to God, he must hear and respond to the gospel (Rom. 10:14-17). The gospel is the good news of Jesus - his life, death, resurrection and his coming kingdom (Q. 66). Through believing the gospel, we receive life and immortality in Christ alone (Q. 67). When a person believes the gospel, they trust fully in the finished work of Christ for salvation on the day of judgment and love him as Savior and Lord (Q. 68).

When a person repents and puts their trust in Christ, having a complete change of heart, it is called being "born again" or "regenerated" (literally "created again"), and only happens by the power of the Holy Spirit (Qs. 70-71). Regeneration is completely in the hand of God and cannot happen by any human effort. This means that salvation cannot be earned in any way. Thus, God's salvation is by grace alone through faith alone in Christ alone (Q. 72; Eph. 2:8-10).

In salvation, therefore, God realizes in Christ a fourfold purpose with respect to believers: their forgiveness, deliverance, reconciliation and progressive growth in holiness, all of which will be finally complete when Jesus returns.

Recommended Resources for this Section:

- Stott, John. *Basic Christianity.*
- Bonhoeffer, Dietrich. *The Cost of Discipleship.*
- Stott, John. *The Cross of Christ.*
- Sproul, R.C. *Chosen by God.*
- Sproul, R.C. *God Alone* DVD.
- Sproul, R.C. *Justified by Faith Alone* DVD.
- Murray, John. *Redemption Accomplished and Applied.*

SAVIOR AND SALVATION

49. Did God leave all humanity under his wrath and the curse of sin?
No, he provided the way of salvation for his elect.

1 Thess. 5:9: *For God has not destined us for wrath, but to obtain salvation through our Lord Jesus Christ ...*

See also Eph. 1:3-7; Rom. 6:23; 8:30; 2 Thess. 2:13-14; 1 Cor. 1:26-31.

50. What is God's only way of salvation?
He sent his Son, Jesus Christ, into the world to save all who believe.

John 3:16: *For God so loved the world, that he gave his only Son, that whoever believes in him should not perish but have eternal life.*

See also Acts 4:12; 1 Tim. 1:15; Heb. 5:9.

51. How did Jesus Christ come into the world?
He was conceived by the Holy Spirit and born of the Virgin Mary.

Matt. 1:23: *"Behold, the virgin shall conceive and bear a son, and they shall call his name Immanuel"* (which means, God with us).

See also Gal. 4:4.

52. What are the two natures of Christ?

He is fully God and fully man.

Col. 2:9: *For in him the whole fullness of deity dwells bodily ...*

See also Gal. 4:4; Phil. 2:5-8.

53. Was Jesus Christ born with original sin?

No, he was born sinless.

Heb. 7:26: *For it was indeed fitting that we should have such a high priest, holy, innocent, unstained, separated from sinners, and exalted above the heavens.*

See also 2 Cor. 5:21; Heb. 4:15; 1 Pet. 2:22.

54. What kind of life did Christ live on earth?

A life of perfect obedience, service and suffering.

1 Peter 2:22: *He committed no sin, neither was deceit found in his mouth.*

See also Matt. 20:28; Heb. 5:8-9; John 8:29; 15:10.

55. How did Jesus satisfy the wrath of God due for your sin?

He became my substitute and made atonement for my sins by his suffering and death.

2 Cor. 5:21: *For our sake he made him to be sin who knew no sin, so that in him we might become the righteousness of God.*

See also Isa. 53:4-5; Rom. 3:25; 4:25; Heb. 2:17; 1 Peter 2:24; 1 John 2:2; 4:10.

56. What kind of death did Jesus die?

A painful and shameful death on the cross.

Phil. 2:8: *And being found in human form, he humbled himself by becoming obedient to the point of death, even death on a cross.*

See also Gal. 3:13; Heb. 12:2.

Section 4: Savior And Salvation

57. What happened on the third day after Jesus died and was buried?

He rose bodily from the dead.

1 Cor. 15:4: *... that he was buried, that he was raised on the third day in accordance with the Scriptures ...*

See also Matt. 28:6; Luke 24:46; Acts 10:40.

58. Where is Jesus now?

He ascended bodily to the right hand of the Father.

Acts 1:9: *And when he had said these things, as they were looking on, he was lifted up, and a cloud took him out of their sight.*

See also Eph. 4:10; John 20:17; Heb. 1:3.

59. Will Jesus return to the earth?

Yes, in the same way that he ascended: in power and glory.

Acts 1:10-11: *And while they were gazing into heaven as he went, behold, two men stood by them in white robes, and said, "Men of Galilee, why do you stand looking into heaven? This Jesus, who was* *taken up from you into heaven, will come in the same way as you saw him go into heaven."*

See also Matt. 24:30; Mark 13:36; John 14:3; Heb. 9:28.

60. Why did Jesus rise from the dead?

To secure justification for all who believe.

Rom. 4:24-25: *... It will be counted to us who believe in him who raised from the dead Jesus our Lord, who was delivered up for our trespasses and raised for our justification.*

See also Isa. 53:5; Rom. 5:18; 8:33-34.

61. What is justification?

God's declaration that all who believe are innocent based on the righteousness of Christ.

Rom. 5:1: *Therefore, since we have been justified by faith, we have peace with God through our Lord Jesus Christ.*

See also Rom. 9:30; 10:9-10; 2 Cor. 5:21; Phil. 3:9; 1 Peter 2:24.

62. How does justification change your relationship with God?

I am no longer God's enemy, but his friend.

John 15:15: *No longer do I call you servants, for the servant does not know what his master is doing; but I have called you friends, for all that I have heard from my Father I have made known to you.*

See also Rom. 5:10; Eph. 2:19.

63. What must you do to be saved?

I must repent of my sin and believe the gospel of Jesus Christ.

Rom. 10:9: *[B]ecause, if you confess with your mouth that Jesus is Lord and believe in your heart that God raised him from the dead, you will be saved.*

See also Mark 1:14-15; Acts 16:30-31.

64. How do you repent of your sin?

I must be sorry for my sin, hate it, turn away from it and turn to God.

1 Thess. 1:9: *For they themselves report concerning us the kind of reception we had among you, and how you turned to God from idols to serve the living and true God ...*

See also Ps. 38:18; Acts 3:19; 26:20; 2 Cor. 7:10.

65. Why must you hate and turn away from sin?

Because sin displeases God.

Isa. 59:2: *[B]ut your iniquities have made a separation between you and your God, and your sins have hidden his face from you so that he does not hear.*

See also 2 Sam. 11:27; Ps. 79:5.

66. What is the gospel?

The good news of Jesus - his life, death, resurrection and his coming kingdom.

Acts 8:12: *But when they believed Philip as he preached good news about the kingdom of God and the name of Jesus Christ, they were baptized, both men and women.*

See also Mark 1:1; Luke 4:43; Acts. 8:12; 1 Peter 1:3-6; 1 Cor. 15:3-4.

67. What does the gospel promise?

Life and immortality in Christ alone.

2 Tim. 1:10: *... and which now has been manifested through the appearing of our Savior Christ Jesus, who abolished death and brought life and immortality to light through the gospel ...*

See also Rom. 2:7; Rev. 2:7; John 17:3.

68. What does it mean to believe the gospel?

To trust fully in the finished work of Christ for salvation on the day of judgment, and to love him as Savior and Lord.

John 14:23: *Jesus answered him, "If anyone loves me, he will keep my word, and my Father will love him, and we will come to him and make our home with him. ..."*

See also Rom. 10:9-10, 16-17; Heb. 11:1; 1 John 4:16-17; 5:4; John 14:21; Titus 3:4-7.

69. Can you repent and trust in Christ by your own power?
No, I cannot repent and believe unless I am born again.

John 3:5: *Jesus answered, "Truly, truly, I say to you, unless one is born of water and the Spirit, he cannot enter the kingdom of God. ..."*

See also 1 Peter 1:3; John 1:12-13; 2 Tim. 2:25; Acts 11:18.

70. What does it mean to be born again?
To experience a complete change of heart, called regeneration.

Titus 3:5: *[God] saved us, not because of works done by us in righteousness, but according to his own mercy, by the washing of regeneration and renewal of the Holy Spirit ...*

See also Ezek. 36:26-27; 2 Cor. 3:18; Col. 2:13; Rom. 7:6.

71. Who can change a sinner's heart?
The Holy Spirit alone.

Rom. 8:1-2: *There is therefore now no condemnation for those who are in Christ Jesus. For the law of the Spirit of life has set you free in Christ Jesus from the law of sin and death.*

See also Matt. 3:11; John 3:5-8; 2 Cor. 3:17-18; 5:7.

72. Can you earn God's salvation in any way?

No, salvation is by grace alone through faith alone in Christ alone.

Gal. 2:16: *[Y]et we know that a person is not justified by works of the law but through faith in Jesus Christ, so we also have believed in Christ Jesus, in order to be justified by faith in Christ and not by works of the law, because by works of the law no one will be justified.*

See also Eph. 2:8-10.

Section 5: Christ and Covenant

Summary

Theologians disagree about how to understand the different ways in which God interacted with mankind throughout the Bible (e.g., dispensations or covenants or both or neither), but Evangelical scholars and pastors agree *en masse* that the Old Testament points forward to the cross. As the early church father Augustine wisely stated, "The new is in the old concealed, and the old is in the new revealed." While Jesus is not in every story of the Old Testament, there is a sense in which he is in every book. After all, the entire drama of redemption is cast around God as the protagonist and his unfolding redemptive plan to save humanity from themselves and from his just wrath against them.

From the moment sin entered into the human race, God promised a victor, the "seed" of the woman (an unusual phrase likely pointing forward to what we now call the virgin birth - the only time in history when a woman can be said to have a "seed" that does not originate from man), a male heir who would crush the serpent's head, but would bruise his heel in the process - pointing forward to the Messiah's temporary death (Gen. 3:15). From this point onward, all humanity would be saved not simply "by faith" in general, but "by faith in the good news" of God's redemptive plan in the future Messiah (Q. 73). Paul understands that God "preached the gospel beforehand to Abraham" (Gal. 3:8). Thus, no fallen human was ever saved by obeying the law as though they could earn God's favor. Instead, they made sacrifices by faith trusting that, though the blood of bulls and goats was inadequate, the act of sacrifice would be an outward expression of an inward faith (1 Sam. 15:22; Ps. 51:16-17; Isa. 1:11).

Why then did God promise in Leviticus 17 that the blood of animals was in fact able to redeem one from sin? Once again, we see that the law was only "a shadow of the things to come, but the substance belongs to Christ" (Col. 2:17; also Heb. 10:1). Old Testament rituals, sacrifices, and holy days and festivals all point to Christ, their true fulfillment (Q. 75).

The term "Christ" is the Greek equivalent to the Old Testament "Messiah," both meaning "anointed." In the Old Testament, prophets, priests and kings were all anointed in their respective positions, and the same is true for Christ as he fulfills all of these offices as well (Q. 76). As Prophet, Jesus is the spokesman for God, revealing his will to us (Q. 77). As Priest, he not only made the perfect sacrifice of himself on the cross, but continues to mediate for us before the throne of grace, praying for us and advocating in our defense (Q. 78; 1 John 2:1). In his role as King, Jesus does not wait for his future kingdom until he rules, but rather he rules even now from heaven over all things and above all powers (Q. 79; Eph. 1:20-22), though the full reality and consummation of his rule still awaits his future return.

While the Bible is one grand story of God's redemptive plan leading to Christ, some have charged God with being inconsistent; that is, the God of the Old Testament is wrathful and angry, but the God of the New Testament is merciful and loving. Nothing could be further from the truth. God's agreement with Israel in the old covenant (Q. 80) was based upon a promise (Q. 81) and a requirement to follow God's law, which they failed to do (Q. 82). That same promise is fulfilled in Christ, who obeyed the law and earned salvation for his people (Q. 83). God is love in the Old Testament, shown by his mercy in not annihilating Israel for disobedience (Ex. 34:6) and accepting imperfect animal sacrifices. God is wrath in the New Testament by pouring out his justice upon Jesus on the cross. God's demands never changed.

This is now reflected in God's new agreement in the new covenant (Q. 84) when he sent Jesus to do what the law was powerless to do (i.e., to bring humanity to salvation; Q. 85). Christians can now not only be free from the curse of the law (Gal. 3:13), but in fact because of Christ, the "righteous requirement of the law might be fulfilled in us" (Rom. 8:3; 3:31). Christians then walk by a new law no less challenging: the law of Christ (Q. 86). Like the Old Testament law, or the Beatitudes, or the parable of the good Samaritan, so it is with the law of Christ; we are constantly reminded of the depths of our depravity and the heights of his glorious grace to draw us near to him (Q. 87).

We are perfect in Christ. However, in this world we will never be perfect in all respects, so Jesus has sent us a helper in our time of need, the Holy Spirit, who seals us for the day of redemption and teaches us to walk with love (Q. 88; Eph. 4:30).

Recommended Resources for this Section:

- Guthrie, Nancy. *Seeing Jesus in the Old Testament*, Vols. 1-5.
- Goldsworthy, Graeme. *According to Plan: The Unfolding Revelation of God in the Bible.*
- Carson, D.A. et al. *The Scriptures Testify about Me: Jesus and the Gospel in the Old Testament.*
- Kaiser, Walter. *The Promise-Plan of God.*

CHRIST AND COVENANT

73. How were sinners saved before the coming of Christ?
By believing in the promised Messiah.

Heb. 11:13: *These all died in faith, not having received the things promised, but having seen them and greeted them from afar, and having acknowledged that they were strangers and exiles on the earth.*

See also Gen. 3:15; Acts 4:12; Rom. 4:1-16; Gal. 3:8; 1 Peter 1:10-12.

74. How did believers show their faith before Christ came?
They offered the sacrifices God required in his law.

Heb. 11:4: *By faith Abel offered to God a more acceptable sacrifice than Cain, through which he was commended as righteous, God commending him by accepting his gifts. And through his faith, though he died, he still speaks.*

See also 1 Sam. 15:22; Ps. 51:16-17; Isa. 1:11; Gal. 3:11; Heb. 10:1, 4; 11:17.

Section 5: Christ And Covenant

75. What did these sacrifices represent?
Christ, the Lamb of God, who would come to die as a substitute for sinners.

John 1:29: *The next day he saw Jesus coming toward him, and said, "Behold, the Lamb of God, who takes away the sin of the world! ..."*

See also 1 Peter 1:19; Rev. 5:9; 13:8; Heb. 9:13-14.

76. What offices does Christ fulfill as the promised Messiah?
Prophet, Priest and King.

Isa. 9:6: *For to us a child is born, to us a son is given; and the government shall be upon his shoulder, and his name shall be called Wonderful Counselor, Mighty God, Everlasting Father, Prince of Peace.*

See also Matt. 21:5; 27:11; Luke 13:31-33; John 8:28; 12:49; 1 Tim. 2:5; Heb. 6:20; 9:11; Rev. 19:11-16.

77. How is Christ your Prophet?
He teaches me the will of God.

Acts 3:22: *"... Moses said, 'The Lord God will raise up for you a prophet like me from your brothers. You shall listen to him in whatever he tells you. ...'"*

See also John 7:16; 17:8; Deut. 18:15.

78. How is Christ your Priest?

He sacrificed himself for my sins and continues to pray for me.

Heb. 2:17: *Therefore he had to be made like his brothers in every respect, so that he might become a merciful and faithful high priest in the service of God, to make propitiation for the sins of the people.*

See also Rom. 8:34; Heb. 7:25; 1 John 2:1.

79. How is Christ your King?

He rules over me, the world and Satan.

Rev. 19:16: *On his robe and on his thigh he has a name written, King of kings and Lord of lords.*

See also Isa. 33:22; Heb. 1:3; Eph. 1:22-23.

80. What is the agreement God made with his people in the Old Testament?

The old covenant.

Ex. 24:7: *Then he took the Book of the Covenant and read it in the hearing of the people. And they said, "All that the LORD has spoken we will do, and we will be obedient."*

See also 2 Cor. 3:14; Heb. 8:6-13; 9:15.

81. What is the promise of the old covenant?

That God would use Abraham to create a nation, called Israel, who would follow his law and bless the whole world.

Gen. 12:2-3: *"... And I will make of you a great nation, and I will bless you and make your name great, so that you will be a blessing. I will bless those who bless you, and him who dishonors you I will curse, and in you all the families of the earth shall be blessed."*

See also Gen. 15:18-21; 17:9-14; Ex. 32:13.

82. Did Israel follow God's law perfectly?

No, God's law showed them how sinful they were and why they needed a Messiah.

Rom. 3:20: *For by works of the law no human being will be justified in his sight, since through the law comes knowledge of sin.*

See also Ps. 14:3; Jer. 31:31-32; Rom. 4:14-15; 5:13, 20; 7:7; 1 Cor. 15:56; Gal. 3:10.

83. Has anyone followed God's law perfectly?

Yes, Christ alone; and through his perfect obedience he earned salvation for me.

Heb. 5:8-9: *Although he was a son, he learned obedience through what he suffered. And being made perfect, he became the source of eternal salvation to all who obey him, ...*

See also Matt. 5:17; Acts 13:39; 2 Cor. 5:21; 1 Peter 2:22; Phil. 2:8.

84. What is the agreement God made with his people through Christ to redeem sinners?

The new covenant.

Jer. 31:31: *Behold, the days are coming, declares the LORD, when I will make a new covenant with the house of Israel and the house of Judah ...*

See also Luke 22:20; 2 Cor. 3:6; Heb. 8:6.

85. What is the promise of the new covenant?

That God will forgive his people through the shed blood of Christ and grant them power to follow the law of Christ by his Spirit.

Matt. 26:28: *"... for this is my blood of the covenant, which is poured out for many for the forgiveness of sins. ..."*

See also Jer. 31:31-32; Rom. 3:31; Col. 1:13-14; 2 Cor. 3:6; Heb. 8:13; 9:15; 12:24.

86. What is the law of Christ?

Love God with all your heart, soul, strength and mind, and love your neighbor as yourself.

Luke 10:27: *And he answered, "You shall love the Lord your God with all your heart and with all your soul and with all your strength and with all your mind, and your neighbor as yourself."*

See also Rom. 13:8; Gal. 5:14; 6:2; James 2:8; 1 Cor. 9:21.

87. Has anyone obeyed the law of Christ perfectly?

Yes, Christ alone; and he gives me help to please him and forgives me when I don't.

Heb. 4:16: *Let us then with confidence draw near to the throne of grace, that we may receive mercy and find grace to help in time of need.*

See also Col. 1:13-14; 1 Peter 2:22.

88. What help did Jesus promise when he ascended?

The Holy Spirit, who would be with us forever.

John 16:7: "... *Nevertheless, I tell you the truth: it is to your advantage that I go away, for if I do not go away, the Helper will not come to you. But if I go, I will send him to you.* ..."

See also Luke 24:49; John 14:16-17, 26; 15:26, 13; Acts 1:4-8; Eph. 4:7-12.

Section 6: Spirit, Sanctification and Scripture

Summary

The Holy Spirit is visibly active throughout the New Testament. In the Gospels, we first see the Spirit descending upon Jesus himself "like a dove" at Jesus' baptism where the fullness of the Trinity is on display (Matt. 3:16; Luke 3:22). The Holy Spirit first indwells Jesus' early followers in full measure at the day of Pentecost, at which time they are able to perform amazing signs and wonders such as speaking in tongues not native to them (Q. 89; Acts 2:1-4).

On at least four occasions in the gospel of John, we read of Jesus' promise of a coming "Helper." This "Helper" - whom we know to be the Holy Spirit - would come only after Jesus' time on earth was complete (John 16:7). He is one whom Jesus promised as a teacher and guide for his followers (Q. 90; John 14:26), as well as a witness concerning the things of Christ (15:26). He is no mere power, but the third person of the Trinity who knows and feels and loves.

In the Old Testament, the Holy Spirit's presence was sporadic, sometimes coming upon someone and then leaving (e.g., Saul, Samson) and at other times a more permanent possession (e.g., David). In the New Testament, however, he continuously abides and permanently indwells all those who sincerely trust Jesus for their salvation (Q. 91). Evidence of the Spirit's presence in one's life is seen by the spiritual fruit he bears (Q. 92).

The work of increasing our spiritual insight, capacity and zeal is called *sanctification*, by which we are set apart and made holy for Christ in this world (Q. 94). The Spirit does this by giving those born in Christ new desires so that they may live out his promises and become more like him (Q. 95). Jesus grew in wisdom and stature, and the same is expected of Christians (Eph. 4:15-19). Jesus depended on his Father and trusted the Spirit, so our dependency must increase as well.

The doctrine of sanctification can be understood in three movements. First, we are viewed by God as already sinless, already perfect and already righteous because of the work of Christ (i.e., positional sanctification). Then, we attempt to live out our identity in Christ by pursuing obedience to Christ and continually being refined by his Spirit (i.e., progressive sanctification; Q. 96). Lastly, when Christ returns, we will be raised imperishable and be complete in Christ (i.e., perfect sanctification).

Christians are promised a position as kings and priests of the Most High God, and yet they will not have arrived at perfect sanctification until Christ returns (Q. 99). Until then, they struggle with and fight against their own sinful flesh (Q. 98), living in what many call the "already, but not yet."

In this world, Jesus said we will have trouble (John 16:33), and our hearts will condemn us (1 John 3:20), but God is greater than both and assures us by his Spirit that we are sons and daughters of the King (Q. 100). We walk in his righteousness. We rule by his power. Every believer is gifted and equipped with spiritual gifts (Q. 101), and the prayerful desire for more (1 Cor. 12:31; 14:1, 39).

One of the most powerful tools the Holy Spirit uses in the life of the believer is the Bible itself (Q. 102). The Bible is the written Word of God, breathed out by him so that it is "living and active, sharper than any two-edged sword, piercing to the division of soul and spirit, of joints and of marrow, and discerning the thoughts and intentions of the heart" (Heb. 4:12; Q. 103).

The Scriptures are breathed out by God as the supernatural product of a divine mind. They reveal his heart and will for his people and carry his absolute, authoritative, conscience-binding, judicial ruling in all matters of faith and practice (Q. 108). Therefore, the Christian must keep it on his lips (Josh. 1:8), eat it and digest it (Ezek. 3:3), and then to do what it says and teach others to do likewise (Q. 109; Ezra 7:10). It is not enough to preach it and teach it, but we must hear it and respond with action, or else our ears are deaf, our eyes blind, our hearts hard and our faith dead (Q. 110; James 1:22-27).

With such a powerful arsenal at each believer's disposal, God has supplied us well with all we need to move forward toward his kingdom, growing stronger each day in him. What more could we ever ask for than the wonderful gift of his Spirit?

Recommended Resources for this Section:

- Piper, John. *Future Grace.*
- Wilkerson, Mike. *Redemption: Freed by Jesus from the Idols We Worship and the Wounds We Carry.*
- DeYoung, Kevin. *Taking God at His Word.*
- Fee, Gordon D., and Douglas Stuart. *How to Read the Bible for All Its Worth.*
- Ferguson, Sinclair. *Who Is the Holy Spirit?* DVD.
- Sproul, R.C. *Pleasing God: Discovering the Meaning and Importance of Sanctification.*
- Wenham, John. *Christ and the Bible,* 3rd edition.
- Owen, John. *Overcoming Sin and Temptation.* Kelly M. Kapic and Justin Taylor, eds.
- Ryle, J.C. *Holiness: Its Nature, Hindrances, Difficulties, and Roots.*
- Peterson, David. *Possessed by God: A New Testament Theology of Sanctification and Holiness.* D.A. Carson, ed.

SPIRIT, SANCTIFICATION AND SCRIPTURE

89. When did the Holy Spirit come?

He came on the day of Pentecost.

Acts 2:1-4: *When the day of Pentecost arrived, they were all together in one place. And suddenly there came from heaven a sound like a mighty rushing wind, and it filled the entire house where they were sitting. And divided tongues as of fire appeared to them and rested on each one of them. And they were all filled with the Holy Spirit and began to speak in other tongues as the Spirit gave them utterance.*

See also Acts 1:5, 8.

90. What did Jesus say the Holy Spirit would do?

He would be their helper and teacher.

John 14:26: *"... But the Helper, the Holy Spirit, whom the Father will send in my name, he will teach you all things and bring to your remembrance all that I have said to you. ..."*

See also John 14:16; 15:26; 16:7-11, 13; 1 John 2:27; 5:6; Rom. 8:26-27.

91. Do you have the Holy Spirit now?
Yes, he lives in me because I have trusted in Christ as Savior and Lord.

Rom. 8:14-15: *For all who are led by the Spirit of God are sons of God. For you did not receive the spirit of slavery to fall back into fear, but you have received the Spirit of adoption as sons, by whom we cry, "Abba! Father!"*

See also John 14:16-17; 1 John 3:24; 4:15; Rom. 5:5; 8:9-11, 16-17; 1 Cor. 6:19-20.

92. How do you know the Holy Spirit lives in you?
Because I see the fruit of his work in my life.

Rom. 5:5: *[A]nd hope does not put us to shame, because God's love has been poured into our hearts through the Holy Spirit who has been given to us.*

See also Matt. 3:8; John 15:8; Rom. 8:14-17; 1 Cor. 2:10-14; Gal. 5:16-26.

93. What is the fruit of the Spirit?
The fruit of the Spirit is love, joy, peace, patience, kindness, goodness, faithfulness, gentleness and self-control.

Section 6: Spirit, Sanctification And Scripture

Gal. 5:22-23: *But the fruit of the Spirit is love, joy, peace, patience, kindness, goodness, faithfulness, gentleness, self-control; against such things there is no law.*

See also Matt. 13:23; Rom. 5:3-5; 12:9-21; Eph. 5:9; 1 Tim. 6:11; 2 Peter 1:5-11; 1 Cor. 13.

94. What do you call the Holy Spirit's work in your life?
Sanctification.

2 Thess. 2:13: *But we ought always to give thanks to God for you, brothers beloved by the Lord, because God chose you as the firstfruits to be saved, through sanctification by the Spirit and belief in the truth.*

See also Rom. 6:19-22; 1 Cor. 1:30; 1 Peter 1:2.

95. How does the Holy Spirit sanctify you?
By giving me a new nature to live out the promises of Christ and to become more like him.

2 Peter 1:4: *... by which he has granted to us his precious and very great promises, so that through them you may become partakers of the divine* nature, having escaped from the corruption that is in the world because of sinful desire.

See also Gal. 5:22-25; Eph. 4:20-24; 2 Cor. 3:18; 1 Thess. 5:23; 2 Peter 1:5-8.

96. What is the effect of this new nature?
I can now make godly choices, think godly thoughts and feel godly feelings.

Gal. 5:24: *And those who belong to Christ Jesus have crucified the flesh with its passions and desires.*

See also Gal. 5:22-25; Eph. 4:20-24.

97. How do I become more like Christ?
By seeing and savoring Jesus in my mind and heart.

2 Cor. 3:18: *And we all, with unveiled face, beholding the glory of the Lord, are being transformed into the same image from one degree of glory to another. For this comes from the Lord who is the Spirit.*

See also Rom. 8:29; Col. 3:10; Heb. 12:2; 1 John 3:2; 1 Cor. 13:12.

98. Why do you still sin?

Because my sinful flesh is at war against the Spirit of God.

Gal. 5:17: *For the desires of the flesh are against the Spirit, and the desires of the Spirit are against the flesh, for these are opposed to each other, to keep you from doing the things you want to do.*

See also 1 Peter 2:11; James 4:1; Rom. 7:5, 15, 18.

99. When will you be fully sanctified?

When Jesus returns and makes all things new.

Phil. 1:6: *And I am sure of this, that he who began a good work in you will bring it to completion at the day of Jesus Christ.*

See also Phil. 3:12; 1 Thess. 5:23-24; 1 John 3:2.

100. How does the Holy Spirit give you assurance of salvation?

He reminds me of my adoption into the family of God and seals me for the day of redemption.

Rom. 8:16: *The Spirit himself bears witness with our spirit that we are children of God, ...*

See also Eph. 1:13; 4:30; 1 John 3:19-20; Rom. 8:14-17.

101. How does the Holy Spirit empower you for service?
By giving me spiritual gifts for building up the church.

1 Cor. 12:4-7: *Now there are varieties of gifts, but the same Spirit; and there are varieties of service, but the same Lord; and there are varieties of activities, but it is the same God who empowers them all in everyone. To each is given the manifestation of the Spirit for the common good.*

See also Rom. 12:3-8; Eph. 2:8-10; 4:7-12; 1 Cor. 12-14; Titus 2:14.

102. In what other ways does the Holy Spirit help me?
The Holy Spirit helps me in prayer and in my study of the Bible.

Rom. 8:26: *Likewise the Spirit helps us in our weakness. For we do not know what to pray for as we ought, but the Spirit himself intercedes for us with groanings too deep for words.*

See also John 16:13; 1 Cor. 2:10-14; 2 Cor. 3:12-18; Eph. 1:17-18.

103. What is the Bible?
The written Word of God, breathed out by him.

2 Tim. 3:16-17: *All Scripture is breathed out by God and profitable for teaching, for reproof, for correction, and for training in righteousness, that the man of God may be complete, equipped for every good work.*

See also 2 Sam. 23:1-2; Jer. 20:9; Luke 1:70; Rom. 1:21; Acts 3:21; Heb. 1:1; 4:12.

104. Who wrote the Bible?

The Holy Spirit through men chosen by God.

2 Peter 1:21: *For no prophecy was ever produced by the will of man, but men spoke from God as they were carried along by the Holy Spirit.*

See also Jer. 1:4-5; Ezek. 18:1; Zech. 4:8; 2 Tim. 3:16-17.

105. Why was the Bible written?

It was written to reveal God and his plan of redemption through Christ.

Luke 24:27: *And beginning with Moses and all the Prophets, he interpreted to them in all the Scriptures the things concerning himself.*

See also Luke 1:1-4; John 20:30-31; Rom. 4:22-25; 5; 15:4; 1 Cor 2:6-16; 10:11; Heb. 1:1-2.

106. How many books are in the Bible?

There are 39 books in the Old Testament and 27 books in the New Testament.

107. Can you trust the Bible?

Yes, because God's Word is truth.

John 17:17: *Sanctify them in the truth; your word is truth.*

See also Ps. 33:4; 119:160; Isa. 40:8; 55:11; Matt. 24:35.

108. Do you need to use the Bible every day?

Yes, because it is my only standard for faith and practice.

Ps. 19:7: *The law of the LORD is perfect, reviving the soul; the testimony of the LORD is sure, making wise the simple; ...*

See also Ps. 1:1-3; 19:7-11; 112:1; 119:15, 48, 97; Josh. 1:8; Matt. 4:4; 2 Tim. 3:16-17.

109. How should you use the Bible personally?

By studying, memorizing, meditating and obeying all it commands through the power of the Holy Spirit.

Ps. 119:9-11: *How can a young man keep his way pure? By guarding it according to your word. With my whole heart I seek you; let me not wander from your commandments! I have stored up your word in my heart, that I might not sin against you.*

See also Josh. 1:8; Ps. 119:27, 44-47; Col. 3:16.

110. How should you use the Bible in Christian community?
By hearing and responding to the Word as it is read and proclaimed.

James 1:22: *But be doers of the word, and not hearers only, deceiving yourselves.*

See also Acts 2:42; Rom. 10:17; 1 Tim. 4:13; 2 Tim. 3:16; 4:2.

Section 7: Community and Kingdom Living

Summary

Throughout the New Testament, we see a glorious picture of salvation – all that God has done to rescue people from sin and death and restore them to himself. But to say that all the New Testament describes is individual salvation is to miss one of its most important emphases. Moreover, to live your life as if all that matters is your personal relationship with the Lord is to miss one of God's most precious gifts.

God's work in this world is to redeem "a people for his own possession" (1 Peter 2:9). This new, redeemed community is what Scripture calls *the church* (Q. 111), and there are several metaphors that are used to describe this (Q. 112).

The New Testament refers to the church in two senses: the universal church and the local church. The universal church refers not to a specific group of believers, but to every true believer from every place and every age. When one confesses

Jesus as Lord and Savior, having been born of the Spirit, he or she is automatically welcomed into Christ's universal church (Q. 113; 1 Cor. 1:2; 12:27).

However, membership in this universal body is intended to be demonstrated in the context of a real commitment to a local church. A group of Christians is not a "church" unless it is an ordered assembly of a specific group of believers in a specific place (Q. 114; Acts 16:5; 1 Cor. 12:20-27; 16:19) with a specific purpose and mission (Qs. 115-116; Matt. 28:19-20; Mark 12:30; 1 Peter 2:9).

The church is also the steward of two symbolic ordinances (Q. 117) that demonstrate the invisible reality of God's grace: believer's baptism (Qs. 118-119) and the Lord's Supper (Qs. 120-122). These two ordinances are open to all believers in Jesus Christ who have repented of their sins and desire to symbolically reenact the truth of the gospel and thereby be moved to a greater understanding and appreciation of all that has been accomplished for them (Q. 123).

The commission that the church has been given (Q. 116) is fulfilled within the local church as the people of God live according to God's design for his community. This can be seen in Acts 2:42 where the church was devoted to teaching, fellowship, breaking of bread and prayer (Qs. 124-127).

Within the context of the committed relationships of the local church, believers in Jesus Christ also enjoy the gift of prayer – the pouring out of one's heart in conversation with God (Q. 127; Lam. 2:19; Ps. 142:1-2). Though often viewed only as an individual and private activity (Matt. 6:6), prayer is also intended to be a corporate activity. Jesus is often seen praying in crowds, teaching his disciples to pray "*our* Father," and after his ascension and throughout the book of Acts, God's people regularly gather for communal prayer.

In light of the entire counsel of Scripture, we see that we are called to pray to God our Father (Q. 128) through the Spirit (Rom. 8:26) in the name of Jesus (Q. 129). To pray in the name of Jesus is to pray according to the will of Jesus (1 John 5:14) revealed in the Word of God and discerned through practice (Rom. 12:2). One way to practice prayer to better understand God's will is to master the pattern given by Jesus (Qs. 131-132; Matt. 6:9-13; Luke 11:1-4).

If the Spirit of the living God resides within us and within our community chosen by Christ, then our lives and our congregations' lives will be marked by love both toward God and toward one another so much so that it spills out to the surrounding culture. By submitting ourselves entirely to the rule of King Jesus, our aim is to glorify God as citizens of his kingdom (Qs. 133-135), persevering while we wait in eager expectation for his return (Q. 136).

Recommended Resources for this Section:

- Bonhoeffer, Dietrich. *Life Together: The Classic Exploration of Christian Community.*

Section 7: Community And Kingdom Living

- Chester, Tim, and Steve Timmis. *Total Church: A Radical Reshaping Around the Gospel and Community.*
  -- *Everyday Church: Gospel Communities on Mission.*
- Keller, Timothy. *Prayer: Experiencing Awe and Intimacy with God.*
- Stedman, Ray C. *Body Life.*
- Banks, Robert. *Going to Church in the First Century.*
- Clowney, Edward. *The Church.*
- Dever, Mark. *The Church: The Gospel Made Visible.*
- Bounds, E.M. *The Complete Works of E.M. Bounds.*
- The Heritage Foundation. *Seek Social Justice: Transforming Lives in Need* DVD.

COMMUNITY AND KINGDOM LIVING

111. What do you call the redeemed community of Christ?
The church.

> **1 Cor. 1:2:** *To the church of God that is in Corinth, to those sanctified in Christ Jesus, called to be saints together with all those who in every place call upon the name of our Lord Jesus Christ, both their Lord and ours: ...*

See also Acts 9:31; Eph. 1:22-23.

112. What are some metaphors for the church?
The body of Christ, the bride of Christ and the household of God.

> **Eph. 1:22-23:** *And he put all things under his feet and gave him as head over all things to the church, which is his body, the fullness of him who fills all in all.*

See also 1 Cor. 12:27; Eph. 2:19; 4:12; 5:25-27; Col. 1:18, 24; 1 Tim. 3:15; Rev. 19:7.

Section 7: Community And Kingdom Living

113. Who are members of the church?

All those who confess Jesus as Lord and Savior, are born of the Spirit, and have been baptized into the name of the Father, Son and Holy Spirit.

1 Cor. 12:12-14: *For just as the body is one and has many members, and all the members of the body, though many, are one body, so it is with Christ. For in one Spirit we were all baptized into one body - Jews or Greeks, slaves or free - and all were made to drink of one Spirit. For the body does not consist of one member but of many.*

See also Matt. 28:18-20; Eph. 4:4-6.

114. What does it mean to be a member of the church?

To be united and accountable to a local, ordered assembly of believers.

Heb. 10:24-25: *And let us consider how to stir up one another to love and good works, not neglecting to meet together, as is the habit of some, but encouraging one another, and all the more as you see the Day drawing near.*

See also 1 Cor. 12:20-27; Heb. 13:17.

115. How do we live as members of Christ's church?
By loving one another as brothers and sisters in the faith.

1 Peter 1:22: *Having purified your souls by your obedience to the truth for a sincere brotherly love, love one another earnestly from a pure heart, ...*

See also Rom. 12:10; Eph. 4:25; Heb. 13:1; 1 John 4:7.

116. What did Jesus commission his church to do?
To make disciples of all nations.

Matt. 28:18-20: *And Jesus came and said to them, "All authority in heaven and on earth has been given to me. Go therefore and make disciples of all nations, baptizing them in the name of the Father and of the Son and of the Holy Spirit, teaching them to observe all that I have commanded you. And behold, I am with you always, to the end of the age."*

See also Mark 12:30; John 4:24; 1 Peter 2:9.

117. What are the two ordinances Jesus gave the church?
Baptism and the Lord's Supper.

Acts 2:41-42: *So those who received his word were baptized, and there were added that day about three thousand souls. And they devoted themselves to the apostles' teaching and the fellowship, to the breaking of bread and the prayers.*

See also Matt. 28:19-20; 1 Cor. 11:23-24.

118. What is baptism?

Baptism is immersion in water in the name of the Father, Son and the Holy Spirit for those who profess personal faith in Jesus Christ.

Acts 2:38: *And Peter said to them, "Repent and be baptized every one of you in the name of Jesus Christ for the forgiveness of your sins, and you will receive the gift of the Holy Spirit. ..."*

See also Matt. 3:16; 28:19-20; Acts 2:36-38; 8:35-36; 16:29-34.

119. What does baptism symbolize?

Union with Christ in his death, burial and resurrection.

Rom. 6:3-5: *Do you not know that all of us who have been baptized into Christ Jesus were baptized* *into his death? We were buried therefore with him by baptism into death, in order that, just as Christ was raised from the dead by the glory of the Father, we too might walk in newness of life. For if we have been united with him in a death like his, we shall certainly be united with him in a resurrection like his.*

See also 1 Cor. 12:13; Col. 2:12; 1 Peter 3:21; Heb. 10:22.

120. What is the Lord's Supper?

The breaking of bread and drinking of wine in remembrance of the sufferings and death of Christ until he returns.

1 Cor. 11:26: *For as often as you eat this bread and drink the cup, you proclaim the Lord's death until he comes.*

See also Matt. 26:26-30; Luke 22:19-20; John 6:35-71; Acts 2:42; 1 Cor. 11:20-25.

121. What does the bread represent?

The body of Christ, broken for our sins.

Matt. 26:26: *Now as they were eating, Jesus took bread, and after blessing it broke it and gave it to the disciples, and said, "Take, eat; this is my body."*

See also 1 Cor. 11:23-24; John 6:35-71.

122. What does the wine represent?

The blood of Christ, poured out for our salvation.

Matt. 26:27-28: *And he took a cup, and when he had given thanks he gave it to them, saying, "Drink of it, all of you, for this is my blood of the covenant, which is poured out for many for the forgiveness of sins. ..."*

See also 1 Cor. 11:23-25; John 6:35-71.

123. Who should be baptized and partake of the Lord's Supper?

All who have truly repented of their sins, who believe in Jesus Christ as Savior and Lord and are willing to do what he teaches.

Acts 16:31-33: *And they said, "Believe in the Lord Jesus, and you will be saved, you and your household." And they spoke the word of the Lord to him and to all who were in his house. And he* took them the same hour of the night and washed their wounds; and he was baptized at once, he and all his family.

See also Acts 2:37-38; 8:36-38; 10:44-48.

124. What is the church devoted to?

The apostles' teaching, the fellowship of the saints, the breaking of bread and to prayer.

Acts 2:42: *And they devoted themselves to the apostles' teaching and the fellowship, to the breaking of bread and the prayers.*

See also Rom. 12:12; 1 Tim 4:16; 2 Tim. 1:13; 1 John 1:6-7.

125. What is the apostles' teaching?

The New Testament commands for belief and behavior in the household of God.

1 Tim. 3:14-15: *I hope to come to you soon, but I am writing these things to you so that, if I delay, you may know how one ought to behave in the household of God, which is the church of the living God, a pillar and buttress of the truth.*

See also Rom. 1:5; 16:17, 26; 1 Cor. 5:9-11; 11:22; 2 Thess. 2:15; 3:6; 1 Tim. 6:3; 2 Tim. 3:10; Titus 1:9.

126. What is fellowship?

Sacrificial love for one another.

Rom. 12:10: *Love one another with brotherly affection. Outdo one another in showing honor.*

See also John 13:34-35; 1 Thess. 4:9; 1 Peter 1:22; 1 John 1:3.

127. What is prayer?

Pouring out my heart in conversation with God.

Lam. 2:19: *"Arise, cry out in the night, at the beginning of the night watches! Pour out your heart like water before the presence of the Lord! Lift your hands to him for the lives of your children, who faint for hunger at the head of every street."*

See also Ps. 18; 62:5-8; 142:1-2; Rom. 8:26; Phil. 4:6-7; Acts 16:25.

128. To whom do you pray?

God, our Heavenly Father.

Matt. 6:9: *Pray then like this: "Our Father in heaven, hallowed be your name. ..."*

See also Luke 22:42; 23:34, 46.

129. In whose name do you ask God to hear and answer your prayers?

In the name of Jesus Christ, his Son.

John 14:13-14: *"... Whatever you ask in my name, this I will do, that the Father may be glorified in the Son. If you ask me anything in my name, I will do it. ..."*

See also John 16:23; 1 John 5:14.

130. Does God answer all prayer?

Yes, according to his wisdom and good pleasure.

1 John 5:14-15: *And this is the confidence that we have toward him, that if we ask anything according to his will he hears us. And if we know that he hears us in whatever we ask, we know that we have the requests that we have asked of him.*

See also Matt. 7:7-11; Rom. 8:26-27.

Section 7: Community And Kingdom Living

131. What pattern has Jesus given to guide the church in prayer?

The Lord's Prayer.

Luke 11:1: *Now Jesus was praying in a certain place, and when he finished, one of his disciples said to him, "Lord, teach us to pray, as John taught his disciples."*

132. What is the Lord's Prayer?

"Our Father in heaven, hallowed be your name. Your kingdom come, your will be done, on earth as it is in heaven. Give us this day our daily bread, and forgive us our debts, as we also have forgiven our debtors. And lead us not into temptation, but deliver us from the evil one. For yours is the kingdom and the power and the glory forever. Amen."

See Matt. 6:9-13; 1 Chron. 29:11.

133. What is your aim as a Christian?

To glorify God as a citizen of his kingdom here on earth.

Phil. 3:20-21: *But our citizenship is in heaven, and from it we await a Savior, the Lord Jesus Christ,* *who will transform our lowly body to be like his glorious body, by the power that enables him even to subject all things to himself.*

See also 1 Cor. 6:20; Col. 3:2-4.

134. How can you glorify God?
By loving him and doing what he commands.

1 John 5:2: *By this we know that we love the children of God, when we love God and obey his commandments.*

See also 1 Sam. 15:22; John 14:15; Rom. 12:1-2.

135. How can you live as a citizen of his kingdom?
By persevering as his chosen possession in this suffering world, eager to do justice, love kindness and walk humbly with my God.

Mic. 6:8: *He has told you, O man, what is good; and what does the LORD require of you but to do justice, and to love kindness, and to walk humbly with your God?*

See also Phil. 3:20-21; Col. 3:2-4; 2 Peter 3:10-14; 1 Peter 2:9; Titus 2:11-14.

136. How do you persevere in the face of suffering?
By clinging to the promises of God and patiently waiting for my blessed hope.

James 5:8: *You also, be patient. Establish your hearts, for the coming of the Lord is at hand.*

See also Mark 10:29-30; John 15:20; 16:33; Acts 5:41; Rom. 5:3-5; 8:17, 36; 2 Cor. 4:7-18; Phil. 1:6; 3:10; 2 Tim. 3:12; James 1:2-4; 1 Peter 4:12; Rev. 2:3.

Section 8: Resurrection

Summary

Death is no respecter of persons, nor does it discriminate on the basis of age, race, status or religion – it is a feature of universal human experience. Indeed, Scripture teaches us in Romans 5:12 that "sin came into the world through one man, and death through sin, and so death spread to all men because all sinned ..." Because of the sin of Adam, death entered the world, and because of the sin of every man and woman since, death remains.

If trusting in Jesus does not prevent this death, what then is the Christian's blessed hope? Many in our culture would answer "life after death," referring to the intermediate state typically pictured as a disembodied soul awaiting the final resurrection. However, when the apostle Paul wanted to offer comfort and encouragement about those who had died so that the Thessalonian Christians would "not grieve as others do who have no hope" (1 Thess. 4:13), he chose instead to talk about the return of Christ when "the dead in Christ will rise first" (v. 16; Q. 137). As one scholar aptly put it, "Christian hope then, is not life after death, but *life after* life after death!"

The exact timing of Christ's return is unknown, but Jesus did predict various signs that he warned his disciples to watch for. For example, he prophesied the destruction of the temple (Luke 21:5-9) and the destruction of Jerusalem (vv. 20-24) - both of which have already come to pass. Christians are called to live with the expectation that Christ is at the doorstep, and therefore to stay awake and be ready (Q. 138).

Bible scholars are not certain whether the New Testament envisions one general resurrection of both the just and the unjust, or whether there are two resurrections: one for believers at the bema seat of Christ (i.e., reward seat; 2 Cor. 5:10) and another for the wicked at the great white throne (Rev. 20:11-15). Whatever the chronology, we are confident that our Lord will raise the dead, judge the world, punish the wicked, reward the righteous and make all things new (Q. 139).

Until that day, all who die are preserved and sustained by the grace of God, not by some intrinsic immortality of the soul (Q. 140). The Christian in particular faces death with an indomitable hope, not that death is an escape from the prison house of the body as Plato taught, but that that they will rise in Christ to victory, blessing and new life (Q. 141). Death is not to be feared, yet it is not welcomed either because it means being spiritually "naked" and "unclothed" as Paul says (2 Cor. 5:3-4), while the soul waits in an unconscious state for its bodily reunion and the full reality of eternal life (Q. 142).

The promise of life and immortality is held out only for those who, in this life, repent of their sin and trust in Jesus Christ. For on the day of Jesus' return, he will judge both the living and the dead. The righteous will receive their reward and the wicked will receive their just punishment. The just punishment for human sin and rebellion against the Creator is eternal destruction (Q. 143; 2 Thess. 1:9). So, on the day of the Lord, they that rejected Christ will be raised bodily from the dead and be condemned to judgment in the lake of fire – a judgment that begins with conscious punishment, but ends with complete annihilation (Q. 144; Rev. 20:11-15). The Scripture's teaching on hell is absolutely clear – it is a place of unimaginable suffering, torment and pain, greatly to be feared. It is, after all, "a fearful thing to fall into the hands of the living God" (Heb. 10:31), the one "who can destroy both soul and body in hell" (Matt. 10:28).

As Christians, we wait in eager expectation for that day when we will finally receive our reward – bodily unto life and immortality with Jesus forever (Q. 145). Paul envisions two phases of resurrection in which we are raised imperishable (likely in our previous bodies), and then changed into complete conformity to Christ (1 Cor. 15:52-56). When Jesus has returned and God's purposes have prevailed, when all believers have been clothed with immortality with bodies that are perfect and imperishable, we shall then live forever in unhindered fellowship with our God in his paradise upon his new earth (Q. 146).

Section 8: Resurrection

Recommended Resources for this Section:

- Wright, N.T. *Surprised by Hope.*
- Dean, David A. *Resurrection Hope.*
- Barton, Freeman. *Heaven, Hell, and Hades.*
- Fudge, Edward. *Hell: A Final Word.*
- Date, Christopher, and Gregory Stump. *Rethinking Hell: Readings in Evangelical Conditionalism.*
- Habermas, Gary R. *The Case for the Resurrection of Jesus.*
- Hewitt, Clarence. *What Does the Future Hold?*

RESURRECTION

137. What is your blessed hope?
That Christ will return, and I will be caught up to live eternally with him on a new earth.

Titus 2:13: *... waiting for our blessed hope, the appearing of the glory of our great God and Savior Jesus Christ, ...*

See also 1 Thess. 4:13-18; Heb. 9:28; Jude 1:21; 2 Peter 3:10-13; Rev. 21.

138. Do you know when Jesus will come back to earth?
No one knows the exact time, but there are signs that it will be soon.

Mark 13:32-33: *"But concerning that day or that hour, no one knows, not even the angels in heaven, nor the Son, but only the Father. Be on guard, keep awake. For you do not know when the time will come. ..."*

See also 1 Thess. 5:2; 2 Peter 3:10; Rev. 1:1, 3, 19; 2:16; 3:11; 4:1; 22:7, 10, 12.

Section 8: Resurrection

139. What will Jesus do when he comes back?

He will raise the dead, judge the world, punish the wicked, reward the righteous and make all things new.

1 Cor. 15:52: ... *in a moment, in the twinkling of an eye, at the last trumpet. For the trumpet will sound, and the dead will be raised imperishable, and we shall be changed.*

See also John 5:29; Rom. 14:10-12; 2 Cor. 5:10-11; 1 Thess. 5:2-3; Rev. 20:10-15; 21:5.

140. What happens to people who die before Christ returns?

The body returns to the dust of the earth and the spirit returns to God.

Eccl. 12:7: *[A]nd the dust returns to the earth as it was, and the spirit returns to God who gave it.*

See also 1 Cor. 15:51; 1 Thess. 4:13-14.

141. How does the Christian face death?

With hope and confidence in the future resurrection through Christ's victory over death.

1 Cor. 15:55-57: *"O death, where is your victory? O death, where is your sting?" The sting of death is sin, and the power of sin is the law. But thanks be to God, who gives us the victory through our Lord Jesus Christ.*

See also 2 Cor. 4:16; 1 Thess. 4:13, 18.

142. Is there any consciousness in death?

No, the dead know nothing.

Eccl. 9:5: *For the living know that they will die, but the dead know nothing, and they have no more reward, for the memory of them is forgotten.*

See also Ps. 6:5; 115:17; Dan. 12:2; Heb. 9:27; Rev 14:13.

143. What is the punishment of the wicked?

Bodily resurrection unto everlasting destruction.

2 Thess. 1:9: *They will suffer the punishment of eternal destruction, away from the presence of the Lord and from the glory of his might, ...*

See also Matt. 25:41, 46; John 5:28-29; Heb. 9:27; 10:29-31.

Section 8: Resurrection

144. What is everlasting destruction?

God's just judgment in the lake of fire leading to complete annihilation.

Rev. 20:14-15: *Then Death and Hades were thrown into the lake of fire. This is the second death, the lake of fire. And if anyone's name was not found written in the book of life, he was thrown into the lake of fire.*

See also Obad. 1:16; Mal. 4:1, 3; Dan. 12:2 with Isa. 66:15-16; Matt. 3:12; 10:28; 13:30; 25:41 with 2 Peter 2:6 and Jude 1:7; 1 Cor 15:26; 2 Thess. 1:5-9; Rev. 14:11 with 18:9-10, 15, 18 and 19:3 esp.; Rev 21:8.

145. What is the reward of the righteous?

Bodily resurrection unto life with Christ forever.

1 Cor. 15:53-54: *For this perishable body must put on the imperishable, and this mortal body must put on immortality. When the perishable puts on the imperishable, and the mortal puts on immortality, then shall come to pass the saying that is written: "Death is swallowed up in victory."*

See also John 5:28-29; Rom. 6:5; 1 Cor. 15:22-23; 2 Tim. 1:10.

146. Where will you be in relationship with Christ for all eternity?

In the new heaven and new earth.

Rev. 21:1: *Then I saw a new heaven and a new earth, for the first heaven and the first earth had passed away, and the sea was no more.*

See also Isa. 65:17; 2 Peter 3:13; Rev. 21:1.

Section 9: New Heaven and New Earth

Summary

While we are given physical descriptions of the new heaven and new earth, we must never lose sight of its symbolic importance as the dwelling place of God with those whom he loves (Q. 147). Jesus refers to this as the kingdom of God and preached about the good news of this coming kingdom (Q. 148). This was the central feature of the gospel message: that Jesus not only died and rose again, but that he would return to set all things right (Acts 1:3; 28:31). In this sense, it is far more than a physical place; it is a reference to God's reign through Christ the King (Q. 149) over all his subjects, the ones given the privilege to eat of the Tree of Life (Q. 150).

After Jesus' ascension into glory to the right hand of God the Father, the angels promised that he would come back in the same way as the disciples saw him leave (Acts 1:9-12). And, according to Zechariah 14:4, it appears that he will even return to the same location – the Mount of Olives. At that time, King Jesus will establish his reign in the renewed city of Jerusalem (Q. 152).

In this new city of God, there is no sun, moon or darkness, for God supplies all the light necessary (Rev. 21:23; 22:5; Isa. 60:19). There is also no sea (Rev. 21:1), but all are sustained by the river of life that flows from the throne of God and the Lamb to the whole city (Rev. 22:1-5). Over this river stands the original Tree of Life denied to Adam and Eve in the garden of Eden, but present now to grant immortality to all who are worthy, and its leaves bring healing to all nations.

Those chosen by God and adopted into his family will "become partakers of the divine nature" (2 Peter 1:4), not only becoming like Christ (1 John 3:2), but even sitting with him on his throne (Rev. 3:21; Eph. 2:6; 2 Tim. 2:12), ruling the millennial nations (Rev. 2:26-27), judging angels (1 Cor. 6:3) and put in charge of many things (Matt. 25:21). Whether one believes in a millennial kingdom that becomes the eternal kingdom or only one, eternal kingdom of God, it will nonetheless be filled with perfect righteousness, peace and joy in the Holy Spirit (Q. 153).

In God's final restoration, those who love Jesus will become holy like him, unable to sin or even desire it (Q. 154). Death, disease, pain and suffering shall be erased as each citizen of the kingdom lives in perfect peace (Q. 155), and even all of creation will benefit from this peace (Q. 156). True, lasting joy beyond the circumstantial happiness of this world will finally spring forth from the most rewarding and satisfying relationship with God and his people for all time (Q. 157).

All this is made possible by the Holy Spirit who indwells his people, soaking everything with the living love that flows from our union with Christ (Q. 158). The promise of the old passing away and the new coming is finally accomplished when God cleanses all with fire - refashioning all things according to his will (Q. 159).

Recommended Resources for this Section:

- Wright, N.T. *New Heavens, New Earth: The Biblical Picture of Christian Hope* (pamphlet).
- Alcorn, Randy. *Heaven.*
- Lloyd-Jones, Martyn. *The Kingdom of God.*
- Wright, N.T. *Surprised by Hope.*
- Beale, G.K., and Mitchell Kim. *God Dwells Among Us: Expanding Eden to the Ends of the Earth.*
- Middleton, J. Richard. *A New Heaven and a New Earth: Reclaiming Biblical Eschatology.*

NEW HEAVEN AND NEW EARTH

147. What is the new heaven and new earth?
The dwelling place of God with his people.

Rev. 21:3: *And I heard a loud voice from the throne saying, "Behold, the dwelling place of God is with man. He will dwell with them, and they will be his people, and God himself will be with them as their God. ..."*

See also Isa. 65:17; 66:22; Rev. 21.

148. What will this new earth be called?
The kingdom of God.

Rev. 11:15: *Then the seventh angel blew his trumpet, and there were loud voices in heaven, saying, "The kingdom of the world has become the kingdom of our Lord and of his Christ, and he shall reign forever and ever."*

See also Matt. 3:2; 10:7; John 18:36; Acts 1:3; 28:31; 1 Cor. 15:50.

149. Who rules as king?
Jesus rules and reigns from his throne.

Rev. 17:14: *"... They will make war on the Lamb, and the Lamb will conquer them, for he is Lord of lords and King of kings, and those with him are called and chosen and faithful.*

See also Rev. 3:21; 5:5-14; 19:16.

150. Who are his subjects?
All those who eat from the Tree of Life in the paradise of God.

Rev. 2:7: *"... 'He who has an ear, let him hear what the Spirit says to the churches. To the one who conquers I will grant to eat of the tree of life, which is in the paradise of God.' ..."*

See also Rev. 3:21; 22:2, 14.

151. What will his subjects do?
Reign with him forever as kings and priests.

Rev. 5:9-10: *And they sang a new song, saying, "Worthy are you to take the scroll and to open its seals, for you were slain, and by your blood you ransomed people for God from every tribe and language and people and nation, and you have made* them a kingdom and priests to our God, and they shall reign on the earth."

See also 2 Tim. 2:11-12; Rev. 2:26-27; 3:21; 20:6; 22:5.

152. From where does he rule?

The New Jerusalem that comes down out of heaven.

Rev. 21:2: *And I saw the holy city, new Jerusalem, coming down out of heaven from God, prepared as a bride adorned for her husband.*

See also Rev. 3:12.

153. What will the kingdom of God be like?

Perfect righteousness, peace and joy in the Holy Spirit.

Rom. 14:17: *For the kingdom of God is not a matter of eating and drinking but of righteousness and peace and joy in the Holy Spirit.*

See also Rom. 5:1-2; 2 Peter 3:13.

154. What does "perfect righteousness" mean?

I become holy and sinless like Christ.

1 John 3:2: *Beloved, we are God's children now, and what we will be has not yet appeared; but we know that when he appears we shall be like him, because we shall see him as he is.*

See also Rom. 8:30; 1 Cor. 1:30; 2 Cor. 5:21; Rev. 21:27.

155. What does "perfect peace" mean?

Christ will wipe away every tear from our eyes, and death shall be no more.

Rev. 21:4: *"... He will wipe away every tear from their eyes, and death shall be no more, neither shall there be mourning, nor crying, nor pain anymore, for the former things have passed away."*

See also Isa. 25:8; 26:3; 35:10; 51:11; 60:20; Jer. 31:12; Phil. 4:6-7.

156. Is this peace only for humans?

No, all creation will be free from sin and reflect God's glory.

Rom. 8:20-21: *For the creation was subjected to futility, not willingly, but because of him who subjected it, in hope that the creation itself will be set free from its bondage to corruption and obtain the freedom of the glory of the children of God.*

See also Isa. 11:6; 65:25; Acts 3:21; Rom. 8:22; Rev. 21:1.

157. What does "perfect joy" mean?

Delighting in my friendship with the triune God and his people for all time.

Ps. 16:11: *You make known to me the path of life; in your presence there is fullness of joy; at your right hand are pleasures forevermore.*

See also Ps. 17:15; 21:6; 23:2, 6; 26:8; 27:4; 36:8; 37:4; 46:4; 63:1-8; John 15:13-15.

158. How will you experience this righteousness, peace and joy?

Through the total indwelling of the Holy Spirit.

1 Cor. 15:44-45: *It is sown a natural body; it is raised a spiritual body. If there is a natural body, there is also a spiritual body. Thus it is written,*

Section 9: New Heaven And New Earth

"The first man Adam became a living being"; the last Adam became a life-giving spirit.

See also Gal. 5:16-25; Rom. 8:1-11; Jer. 31:33; Ezek. 36:26-27.

159. What is God going to do with the old, sinful earth?
He will cleanse it by fire and make all things new when Jesus returns.

2 Peter 3:10: *But the day of the Lord will come like a thief, and then the heavens will pass away with a roar, and the heavenly bodies will be burned up and dissolved, and the earth and the works that are done on it will be exposed.*

See also Ps. 102:25-26; 2 Peter 3:7; Rev. 21:5.

160. In light of this blessed hope, how shall you now live?
I must seek the kingdom of God with all my life as I behold his Son and live by his Spirit with holiness, godliness and zeal.

2 Peter 3:11-14: *Since all these things are thus to be dissolved, what sort of people ought you to be in lives of holiness and godliness, waiting for and hastening the coming of the day of God, because of* *which the heavens will be set on fire and dissolved, and the heavenly bodies will melt as they burn! But according to his promise we are waiting for new heavens and a new earth in which righteousness dwells. Therefore, beloved, since you are waiting for these, be diligent to be found by him without spot or blemish, and at peace.*

See also Isa. 58:10; Acts 20:35; James 4:4; 1 Cor. 15:51-58; 2 Cor. 3:18; Titus 2; 2 Tim. 1:6; 2:22; Eph. 2:10; 4:17-32; Col. 3; 2 Peter. 1:5-15; 1 John 2:15-17.

PART 3 - USING THE CATECHISM IN THE FAMILY
A Suggested Plan for Families

Since it takes time and repetition to learn the catechism, we suggest a three-year cycle with the goal of memorizing one question and one verse once a week. In order to accomplish this, families need at least three drill sessions each week, depending on the child's own ability. The basic outline below offers a walk-through for each question.

Family Devotional Guide

1. **Ready your mind** - Parents read the section introduction themselves, along with the question/answer, and any glossary terms so that they understand the larger theme, and then devise a preparation question for their child.
2. **Reveal the question/answer** - Parents read the question/answer three times aloud and ask their child questions about the words or concepts to make sure they understand the question.

3. **Read the verse** - Parents read the verse aloud three times.
4. **React to God's Word** - Parents ask questions about the verse to ensure comprehension.
5. **Respond with action** - Parents come up with a simple homework exercise to help reinforce the concept (this may be the same homework for the whole week). Write in a journal, help others, volunteer to do a task, create something, etc.

Day 1 (SAMPLE)

1. **Ready your mind** - Today we are going to talk about satisfaction. What satisfies you? What kind of food satisfies you? What kind of activities?
2. **Reveal the question/answer** - Parents read the question/answer aloud three times.

Q. 1: What is your supreme satisfaction in this age and the age to come?

To know and be known by God now and forevermore in the new heaven and the new earth.

What does each of the words mean: "supreme," "satisfaction," "this age," "the age to come"? What does it mean to "know" someone? What does it mean to be "known by someone"? What is the "new heaven and new earth"?

3. **Read the verse** - Parents read the verse aloud three times. **John 17:3:** *And this is eternal life, that they know you the only true God and Jesus Christ whom you have sent.*

4. **React to God's Word** - How is John's definition of eternal life different from how we typically define it? What is the difference between knowing about someone and knowing them? Does John have one of these in mind or both of these?

5. **Respond with action** - Write out a prayer asking the Lord to be your supreme satisfaction, to change your heart and desires so you enjoy him more than the things of the world.

Day 2 (SAMPLE)
* note changes to points 2, 4 below

1. **Ready your mind** - The Family Worship Guide offers a brief introduction for each day, but after the first day, parents may want to skip this step unless they find that a few preparation questions are helpful to get their student focused.

2. **Review the question/answer** - Parents read the question/answer three times aloud then use the blank method to aid in memory retention.

   Recite the answer blanking out one word and letting your student fill in the blank verbally. Some parents find it helpful to use a whiteboard, write the answer and erase the key word replacing it with an underline. For example:

   To know and be known by _____ now and forevermore in the new heaven and the new _____.
   (repeat twice)

   To know and be known by _____ now and _____ in the new _____ and the new ___.
   (repeat twice)

   To _____ and be _____ by _____ now and _____ in the new _____ and the new _____.
   (repeat twice)

3. **Read the verse** - Parents read the verse aloud three times and ask for their students to recite as much of it as possible three times.
4. **React to God's Word** - Parents may choose to read the verse in its chapter context, to listen to the entire chapter using an audio Bible (children enjoy hearing the Bible),

to ask more questions about the verse or to use this time to illustrate the verse with a select Bible story. This is a good exercise for parents as it causes them to have to think deeply about the catechism question and troll their mind for all that they have been taught in order to connect this truth with a biblical illustration. Here is a short sample list:

Question	Suggested Bible Reinforcement (Example)
Q. 1	Dan. 1; 2; 3; 5; 6
Q. 2	Gen. 1-2; Matthew 3:13-17; Acts 4:23-31 (notice "God" in v. 24; "Jesus" in vv. 27, 30; "Holy Spirit" in vv. 25, 31)
Q. 3	Ex. 3; 7-11; Rev. 21
Q. 4	Mark 4:35-41; 14:22-33
Q. 33	Watch or retell the story of Nemo disobeying his father and the consequences that followed.
Q. 44	Go online and type in "10 commandment hand signals" to teach your children.
Q. 93	Go online and find a song about the fruit of the Spirit and spend time learning that.

5. **Respond with action** - Parents come up with a simple homework exercise to help reinforce the concept (this may be the same homework for the whole week). Write in a journal, write a prayer, help others, volunteer to do a task, create something, create something, etc.

Day 3 (SAMPLE)

* note changes to point 2 below

1. **Ready your mind** - Use the Family Worship Guide or skip this step.
2. **Remember the answer** - Parents ask the question and see how much the student can recall. They then read the question/answer three times aloud and use the blank method aiming for complete memorization (more than three days may be needed).
3. **Read the verse** - Parents ask the child to recall as much of the verse as possible, offering perhaps the first word or two. Then, read the verse aloud three times and ask for their children to recite as much of it as possible three times. If the verse is not fully committed to memory at this point, apply the blank method above.
4. **React to God's Word** - Parents should illustrate the question/answer with a Bible story, parable, psalm, etc.
5. **Respond with action.** Parents come up with a simple homework exercise to help reinforce the concept.

Parents should think seriously about the importance of a regular schedule of family worship where Dad leads and everyone participates and praises the Lord through song (e.g., hymn books, YouTube, iPods) and prayer. This is the perfect setting for catechesis and practicing the above outline.

A Suggested Plan For Families

The versatility of catechism for families is that, once everyone is involved in the process, it can be used anywhere. Driving in the car need not be a place to turn on the radio and zone out or for kids to become zombified before a screen. Ask questions and seek answers in a way that honors Deuteronomy chapter six and God's method of child training.

Parents can and should come up with simple games to play using catechism. Score points, form teams and compete or assign children to create their own flashcards on quizlet.com and use their "scatter" feature to compete to see who can match up the question/answer and verses the fastest.

Parents who practice catechism often report feeling ill-equipped. For too long they have pushed this grand privilege off to "the experts," even though God calls them to carry this torch themselves. An easy solution is for parents to begin learning more and learning deeper. Visit biblicaltraining.org and look for "52 Major Stories of the Bible" by Bill Mounce to get started for free. The site is filled with 10-30-hour lectures for deeper learning.

Helpful Resources

About Family Worship

- Baucham, Voddie. *Family Driven Faith.*
- Helopoulos, Jason. *A Neglected Grace: Family Worship in the Christian Home.*
- Beeke, Joel. *Family Worship.*
- Whitney, Donald. *Family Worship.*

For Family Worship

- *Seeds Family Worship* (http://www.seedsfamilyworship.com/).
- *Songs for Saplings* (http://songsforsaplings.com/).
- Lloyd-Jones, Sally. *The Jesus Storybook Bible: Every Story Whispers His Name.*
- Machowski, Marty. *The Gospel Story Bible: Discovering Jesus in the Old and New Testaments.*
- Machowski, Marty. *Long Story Short* and *Old Story New.*
- Erisman, Ken. *Grounded in the Faith: An Essential Guide to Knowing What You Believe and Why.*
- Bennett, Arthur. *The Valley of Vision: A Collection of Puritan Prayers & Devotions.*

PART 4 - USING THE CATECHISM IN THE FAMILY OF GOD
Suggestions for Churches

This catechism is designed to be adaptable and customizable according to diverse church situations. It can accommodate a Pre-K-fourth grade curriculum, fourth-eighth grade, ninth-12th grade or adults. It can be used for church membership or in baptism classes. It can be compacted to fit a pastor's Sunday morning message to kids, to junior church, after-school Bible clubs and summer Bible day camps.

It is vital to understand that the purpose of a catechism is to put a practical tool in the hands of parents. If a church chooses to use this more formally as in the curriculum, we suggest using the first day of Sunday school as a parent orientation where you hand out the "What Is a Catechism?" section. Catechism puts responsibility on parents to train at home multiple days. Parents who do not do this will be obvious to all since their children will not know the weekly question/answer and verse. This is far different from the typical Sunday school program, which requires nothing of the parents.

In any case and in any format, the basic W.I.S.E. structure can provide what a church needs to build a curriculum of its own around each question, whether for 20 minutes or an hour.

- **Wonder** - spike curiosity, introduce the basic idea, activate prior knowledge.
- **Investigate** - study words, concepts, Scripture verses.
- **Seek** - seek for further understanding in the Scriptures, personal life stories, the news, movies, etc.
- **Engage** - do hands-on crafts, visual aids, audible drilling exercises, etc.

Suppose a pastor is preaching on prayer. He calls the children up for a kids' point and shows them a picture or uses an object lesson to immediately capture their interest, and then asks them to interpret it as it relates to prayer (Wonder). He then asks "What is prayer?" (Q. 127) and answers, "Pouring out your heart in conversation with God." He then probes the kids, asking them what "pouring out one's heart" means, and what "conversation with God" means (Investigate). Then, he shares the context of Jeremiah's lament in the key verse; how Israel was rebellious, punished, came to the end of her self-sufficiency and cried out to God; how God responded with prophets and promised that he would one day restore Israel's fortunes (Search). Lastly, the pastor drills the students using the blank method, and then drills each student in succession until they all repeat the answer

(Engage). Perhaps if they can memorize the verse with their parents, he will offer a reward the next week. Or, he assigns an engaging homework assignment such as making a collage of pictures of people praying and pouring out their hearts (Engage).

Churches should have their elders, deacons, boards or Sunday school superintendents review the full curriculum and condense or expand a particular lesson as needed according to their very own context. Once again, it is crucial that parents take responsibility to be involved, engaged and on board with this paradigm if it is to be successful. We recommend asking all families to read Voddie Baucham's *Family Driven Faith* prior to the beginning of classes. The pastor or appointed leaders can host at least one discussion about the book to further spur discussion and commitment by parents. It is not necessary that everyone agrees with every tenet of the book, but that they read it, think about their own family theology and begin to form convictions about how to grow, nurture and strengthen their own children in the Lord.

In addition, the pastor should seriously consider preaching a few topical sermons on the importance of catechism, and then demonstrate its relevance by using it to answer various questions in a sermon.

After an initial preaching event on the topic, the challenge is for the pastor to continue to incorporate the catechism questions into his messages year-round. As he cites a question, he may ask if any children in the congregation know the answer and give them an opportunity to speak during the sermon. This will give students a chance to show what they know, and place healthy pressure on parents to be diligent about training at home. Churches are called to support and empower parents, not supplant them. When churches come alongside parents, they can unleash them for God's glory.

PART 5 - ADDITIONAL RESOURCES
Annotated Glossary

Adoption (Q. 100) - God's act of welcoming sinful human beings into his spiritual family as sons and daughters. To be adopted into God's family means to enjoy all of the rights and privileges of being a child of the King. Every human being was an enemy of God and a slave to sin, but those who trust in Christ experience the freedom of sonship (Rom. 8:14-15; 1 John 3:1-2).

Annihilation (Q. 144) - the complete destruction of the wicked in hell. Both body and soul of the resurrected unbeliever are thrown into hell (the lake of fire) and completely burned up over a period of time. This involves a period of pain, anguish and torment, but eventually ends with the entire destruction of the individual (Matt. 10:28).

Apostles' Teaching (Q. 124) - the New Testament commands for belief and behavior in the household of God. The apostles were 11 men chosen by Christ plus one (Matthias) chosen by lot to take the place of Judas (Matt. 10:2-4; Acts 1:20-26), who witnessed the resurrected Christ. They were commissioned to go into the world and be his witnesses. Their teaching encompassed both orthodoxy (i.e., right belief; John 1:1-4; Titus 1:9) and orthopraxy (i.e., right behavior; hence "teaching them to observe" in Matt. 28:19-20). It also included the blueprint design for Christ's church structured with deacons and elders (thus 1 Tim. 3:14, where Paul refers to his entire letter; esp. vv. 1-13). It became known as a body of cognitive and practical traditions passed on through the ages, much of which is recorded in our New Testament (i.e., traditions of Christ [2 Thess. 2:15; 3:6; 1 Cor. 11:2], not traditions of man [Matt. 15:3; Col. 2:8]).

Atonement (Q. 55) - God's work of reconciling us to himself through Christ (1 John 2:2). All sin is ultimately against God (Ps. 51:4) and separates us from him (Isa. 59:2) so that his holy wrath remains on and increases against us (John 3:36; Rom. 1:18; 2:5). Jesus died in our place, however, paying the penalty for our sins (Rom. 6:23), and in doing so, he satisfied the wrath of God (i.e., propitiation). Christ's death cleanses us from the guilt and stain of sin (i.e., expiation), thus granting forgiveness (Matt. 26:28) and reconciliation to all who believe (Rom. 5:11). In the Old Testament, God appointed an annual "Day of Atonement" for the entire nation of Israel (Lev. 16:29-30; 23:27-28). The people were to bring an innocent animal to sacrifice, the blood subsequently being sprinkled upon the atonement cover of the ark of the covenant as a symbolic way to cover the offenders' sins so that fellowship with God could continue unabated. It is important to note that we cannot be reconciled to God by our own power - he must do the work for us.

Attribute (Q. 9) - a quality or characteristic. In classic theology, God's attributes are understood as incommunicable (things he alone possesses innately) and communicable (things that he shares with humanity). These distinctions are only made to help us comprehend God's infinite majesty, though all distinctions are ultimately inadequate to describe his grandeur. Examples of God's incommunicable attributes are his holiness (Rev. 15:4), immutability (i.e., he never changes; Ps. 90:2; Mal. 3:6; Heb. 13:8), omnipotence (i.e., he is all powerful; Ps. 33:9; Isa. 40:28; 46:10), omnipresence (i.e., he is everywhere; Ps. 139:7-12; Jer. 23:24) and omniscience (i.e., he knows all things; Rom. 16:27; Heb. 4:13; 1 John 3:20). Examples of his communicable attributes are his goodness, love, justice, mercy and knowledge that he bestows on humanity.

Bodily Resurrection (Q. 143) - At the second coming of Jesus Christ, all people, both believers and wicked, will be brought back to physical life from the grave. They will be in their physical bodies at the resurrection. The wicked will be then thrown into the lake of fire and the believers will be given new bodies clothed in immortality (1 Cor. 15; 1 Thess. 4:13-18).

Breathed Out (Q. 103) - the phrase used in 2 Timothy 3:16 to describe the source of all Scripture, translated from the Greek word *theopneustos*, which literally means "God-breathed." This means that every bit of Scripture (the original documents, not subsequent copies and translations) was given by God, using human authors to reveal his will (2 Peter 1:19-21). Because Scripture is breathed out by God, it is "living and active" (Heb. 4:12) and perfectly true in all it intends to teach (John 17:17; Ps. 19:7; Prov. 30:5).

Caught Up (Q. 137) - the idea of rising to meet Jesus at his return, found in 1 Thessalonians 4:17. The Latin Vulgate translates the word "caught up" as *rapiemur*, to which our English terms "rapture" and "raptured" are related. There is a great deal of debate concerning when the rapture occurs. Some argue it is before the great tribulation (pre-tribulation view) that is then followed by a final return of Jesus at a later point. Some contend instead that there are not two returns of Christ, but he comes only once after the tribulation (post-tribulation view) to establish his thousand-year kingdom. Others see no future tribulation at all, so when Jesus returns, he does so fully in his eternal kingdom (Amillennialism). One thing is sure, he does return to reign on a new heaven and new earth at some point. Interestingly, Paul does give us a hint as to the proper interpretation of 1 Thessalonians chapter four when he says we fly up to "meet" the Lord. The term "meet" (*apantesis*) came to be a technical word used in Greek culture to describe a city sending out a welcoming party to honor dignitaries, kings or important persons, and then *return* back into the city with them. Thus, presumably the bridesmaids rush out to meet the bridegroom and return with him (Matt. 25:1, 6). Similarly, using a different but interchangeable word (*upantesis*), the crowds rush out to meet Jesus with palm branches, and then accompany him into the city (John 12:13). In all likelihood, this is Paul's intention as well. (see Gary Shogren, 1 and 2 Thessalonians in the *Zondervan Exegetical Commentary on the New Testament*.)

Conscience (Q. 46) - the inner voice imprinted on humanity as part of being made in the image of God. Even in its fallen, sinful state, it nonetheless points like a moral compass in the direction of God's law written on the human heart (Rom. 2:15). A good conscience is one that honors God (1 Tim. 1:4-5, 18-19), but non-Christians only have a defiled conscience before their Creator (Titus 1:15). If it is ignored long enough, it can become severed (literally "cauterized") so that it no longer pricks the soul (1 Tim. 4:2; Matt. 24:12). Additionally, Christians may possess a weak conscience that is overly sensitive and easily wounded when other Christians attempt to exercise their moral liberties in Christ (e.g., drinking alcohol, the celebration of special holidays, how holy to treat Sunday). A strong conscience, however, understands freedom in Christ and its appropriate boundaries (1 Cor. 8; 10; Rom. 14:1-2).

Counselor (Q. 5) – one of the roles of the Holy Spirit. While God (Ps. 16:7; 32:8; 33:11; 73:24) and Jesus (1 John 2:1; Isa. 9:6) can both be understood as counselors, the main role in the New Testament belongs to the Spirit of God (John 16:7; 14:16). He "counsels" us primarily with biblical wisdom, teaching us about Christ (John 14:26; 15:26; 1 John 2:27), our adoption into the family of God (Rom. 8:14-17; Gal. 4:6) and especially God's love (Rom. 5:5). He produces in us the fruit of righteousness (Gal. 5:22-23) as well as provides power over sin to walk by the Spirit and not gratify the desires of the sinful flesh (Gal. 5:16). Failure to listen to his counsel can grieve him (Eph. 4:30; 1 Thess. 5:19; Heb. 10:29), but surrendering to King Jesus brings fresh fillings of his grace, power and presence in our lives (Eph. 5:17-19).

Day of Judgment (Q. 68) – (also the last judgment, final judgment, day of the Lord) the final climactic return of King Jesus, who will judge the living and the dead as they give an account of their life before him (Acts 10:42; 2 Tim. 4:1; 1 Peter 4:5). Those who trust in Jesus Christ's finished work on the cross and love their Savior will be ushered into eternal life (Matt. 25:46; 2 Tim. 4:8). Those who have rejected and rebelled against him will be sentenced to eternal destruction (Matt. 25:46; 2 Thess. 1:9; Rom. 2:5). The decision to humbly submit to King Jesus must be made *before* that fateful day, for upon that day, all prior decisions will be final without any prospect of second chances.

Exactly when this occurs is a matter of some debate. Some believe this all occurs simultaneously upon the Lord's return; that there is one final, general resurrection and judgment in which believers and nonbelievers are separated and the eternal kingdom on earth is established (Amillennialism). Others understand two resurrections: the first resurrection for the just when Christ returns to usher in his thousand-year rule on earth and to reward the righteous, and a second resurrection after the millennial kingdom in which the wicked are sentenced to the lake of fire (Premillennialism). Still others believe in, essentially, three resurrections. First, a special rapture, whereby some of God's saints are raised and taken. Then, years after the end time tribulation, a second resurrection of all the saints of God take place, which commences the bringing of Christ's millennial kingdom to earth. And, finally, after this thousand-year reign, a general resurrection for the wicked at the end (Dispensationalism). Regardless of one's view on the millennium, the Lord Jesus will return and reign supreme, on this all biblical camps can agree. (Read Dan. 12:1-2; John 5:28-29; 1 Thess. 4:16; Rev. 20:4-5; 20:12-13; 22:12; Rom. 14:10-12; 2 Cor. 5:10; 1 Cor. 3:10-15; Luke 14:14.)

Elect (Q. 49) - God's people, chosen "before the foundation of the world, that we should be holy and blameless before him" (Eph. 1:4; see also 2 Thess. 2:13; 2 Tim. 1:9). God's elect are drawn by the Father to himself (John 6:44; Matt. 22:14). Those that respond to the voice of Jesus are his sheep (John 10:14, 16, 27; 15:16) and nothing can snatch them out of his hand or separate them from his love (John 10:28; Rom. 8:31-39; Matt. 24:24). They persevere to the end because of the energy of Christ that so powerfully works in them "both to will and to work for his good pleasure" (Phil. 2:13; see also Col. 1:29; 1 Cor. 15:10). The controversial aspect of God's election lies in how and in what manner God chooses those who will be saved. Namely, does he look down the corridor of time and see who responds faithfully to his call and then elects them, or does he elect them before they have done anything good or bad? Either way, the vocabulary of "elect" and "chosen" is biblical. (For more on this, see *Why I Am Not an Arminian* by Robert Peterson and *Why I Am Not a Calvinist* by Jerry L. Walls.)

Eternal (Q. 11) - an incommunicable attribute of God by which God always was, is and will be (Rev. 4:8). He had no beginning and he will have no end (Gen. 1:1; Ps. 93:2; Isa. 43:10-13; Rev. 1:8). In this respect, while his infinity is a different category here, he is infinite with respect to time - thus he sees all time simultaneously (2 Peter 3:8).

Faith (Q. 72) - the object of saving faith is Jesus Christ not ourselves, our righteous works (Titus 3:5) or even our own faith. True faith and false faith must be distinguished. True faith has three aspects: *know, agree, trust.* We must *know* who Jesus is (Rom. 10:14-17) before we can place faith in him. We must then *agree* or assent that he is who he claimed to be - the Son of God, the promised Savior. These two aspects are not enough, however, to save anyone. Demons believe these two things and even have a response to them (James 2:19). The key is the last aspect: We must *trust* that Jesus' work of living a sinless life, dying a substitutionary death and rising from the dead will indeed be enough to save us, redeem us and cause us to rise from the dead when he returns as well.

Faith always results in love and good deeds that prove one to be a devout follower of Christ (Heb. 10:24; John 15:8). Good works are the fruit, not the root of saving faith. If there is no transformation, then there is no genuine trust either. Some look like they have experienced true faith, felt the Spirit's power and confessed Jesus only to turn away from him (Heb. 6:4-6). Did they lose their faith? By no means; rather, they never had true, saving faith in the first place, but only ever produced thorns and thistles (vv. 7-8). Dead faith is not no faith - it is an empty and fruitless faith (James 2) that bears no crop (Matt. 13:1-43). True faith cannot be lost because it is a gift of God in the first place, given by his grace and exercised by our regenerated will (Eph. 2:8-9; 2 Peter 1:1; Phil. 1:29; Acts 3:16).

Family of God (Q. 100) - all those who trust in Jesus Christ (Eph. 2:19; 1 Tim. 3:15). The family/household metaphor for the church is a predominant metaphor throughout the New Testament, with believers in Christ knit together as brothers and sisters with God as their Father. The dozens of "one another" verses in Scripture (e.g., love one another, be at peace with one another, do good for one another) do not refer to a love for all humanity *per se*, but to a special love toward our brothers and sisters in Christ. Such devotion to one another in Acts is blessed by God, as he added to their number those that were being saved (2:41, 47; 4:4; 5:14; 6:7; 9:31; 11:21). Local churches are to be a visible display of the relationships within God's household.

Finished Work of Christ (Q. 68) - Christ's perfect life of obedience to the Father leading up to his death and his subsequent resurrection, the focal point of which is his substitutionary atonement on the cross. Through this work, Jesus took upon himself the wrath of God due for our sin, reconciled us to the Father and credited to all who believe his perfect righteousness. The work that the Father gave his Son to do was fully completed, never to be repeated nor added to, so that Jesus could declare from the cross, "It is finished" (John 19:30). Thus, all who trust in his complete work are freed from both the penalty of sin and its power to rule them. The past work of Christ is distinguished from the present work of Christ by his ascension to glory and his continual intercession for the saints. It is here that he applies his finished work to his people as their advocate before the throne of God.

God's Image (Q. 21) - seen in both male and female when they are joined together to create a one-flesh union capable of developing complex relationships, thinking rationally and feeling emotionally.

Grace (Q. 72) - the unearned, undeserved, free gift of God's salvation according to his own good pleasure (Eph. 2:8-10; 1:5; Phil. 2:12-13). God's favor and kindness for us in Christ Jesus can only be understood against the backdrop of sin and his holy anger against it. Since all have sinned and fallen short of his perfect standard (Rom. 3:23), God is just to give humanity what it deserves - namely, death (Rom. 6:23). Instead, he freely provides his Son and opens his arms to all who repent of their sins and turn to him. He saves, adopts, empowers, provides for and promises a future eternal glory, a crown of righteousness earned by his Son and given to us without payment.

Helper (Q. 90) - See "Counselor" above.

Holy (Q. 10) - set apart. Because God is holy, he stands above all so-called gods of this world (first commandment), cannot be represented with wood and silver (second commandment), demands that his name be honored above all as sacred rather than slandered as secular (third commandment) and expects his people to strive to be likewise set apart from the things of this world (fourth-10th commandment; Lev. 19:2). In this last sense, God's people are both set apart and consecrated for his purpose. They are not innately holy, but they become holy because of dedication to him. So, the tabernacle is holy, sacrifices are holy and utensils are holy because they are both set apart and consecrated for God's purpose.

Immortality (Q. 24) - the inability to cease to exist or the ability to exist eternally. The soul of man is not intrinsically immortal. The soul becomes extrinsically immortal upon the reception of everlasting life through faith in Jesus Christ by the will and power of God. All humans, whether righteous or wicked, are subject to physical and spiritual death as a consequence of sin and are universally mortal. Adam and Eve were given the opportunity for immortality if they obeyed God and did not eat from the Tree of the Knowledge of Good and Evil. When they ate from the forbidden tree, they forfeited their access to the Tree of Life, and therefore their ability to live forever.

Indwelling (Q. 158) - the Holy Spirit dwelling inside all true believers; i.e., he is permanently present in the believer's mind, heart, soul, etc. Also see Question 91.

Infinite (Q. 11) - an incommunicable attribute of God by which he is uncontainable and unlimited in his very nature and essence (1 Kings 8:27; Ps. 139:7-12; 147:5; Jer. 23:23-24; Isa. 66:1). This includes his omnipresence, immanence and transcendence.

Justification (Q. 61) - the legal declaration that Christians are righteous and innocent before the throne of grace based solely on the work of Christ. This is a past tense reality (Rom. 5:1), won for us once for all (Heb. 10:1-18). But after being saved, our daily sins are still offensive to our most holy God, and Satan remains our accuser. Thus, justification is a present declaration applied to us over and over again as Christ intercedes for us (Rom. 3:24, 28; Gal. 3:8, 11; Acts 13:39; Rom. 8:34; Heb. 7:24-25; 1 John 2:1). Lastly, it remains as a final, future hope - not by works, but by faith in the Son of God (Rom. 3:20; 2:13). It is important to note that faith does not cause or contribute to justification. Saving faith can only receive God's declaration and respond by walking in the freedom that Christ has won (Gal. 5:1).

Kingdom (Q. 66) - God's divine, kingly reign as proclaimed and inaugurated by Jesus' life, ministry, death and resurrection, and the subsequent outpouring of the Spirit into the world. Jesus is reigning now, and the kingdom of God has arrived. At the same time, we await the future consummation of the divine reign of Jesus when he will dwell physically with us in the new heaven and new earth.

Lake of Fire (Q. 144) - the place where unbelievers meet their final torment and eventual destruction, pictured as a lake of burning sulfur and often referred to today as "hell" (Rev. 21:8). It depicts what final punishment is *like*, but not necessarily all that it entails in terms of its spiritual, emotional and physical horrors. Jesus portrays hell as disobedient servants receiving various beatings (Luke 12:47-48), wicked servants who are cut in pieces (Matt. 24:48-51) and outer darkness (Matt. 8:12; 22:13). John describes it as "the second death" (Rev. 2:11; 20:6, 14-15) and as a pit (Rev. 20:3). By far, the most frequent image, however, is fire as in "eternal fire" (Matt. 25:41), "unquenchable fire" (Mark 9:43; Matt. 3:12) and "fiery furnace" (Matt. 13:42, 50).

The English word "hell" translates three Greek words: (1) *Gehenna*, Jesus' referent to the *future* lake of fire (Mark 9:43; Matt. 5:22, 29-30; 10:28; 18:9), (2) *Hades*, the *present* intermediate realm of the dead equivalent to the Old Testament *sheol*, referring to the grave and resting place of souls that will eventually be emptied into the future Gehenna (Rev. 20:13-14), and (3) *Tartaroo*, used only once to describe the prison of some of the fallen angels (2 Peter 2:4).

Law (Q. 33) - either God's moral law written on the human heart and conscience (Rom. 2:14-15; James 4:17), the Ten Commandments or, more broadly, the first five books of the Old Testament (Pentateuch or Torah) and the laws therein. Here, the reference is especially to the moral law imprinted on humanity as part of being made in the image of God.

Messiah (Q. 4) - from the Hebrew word *masiah*, meaning "anointed one." It refers to the future anointed ruler destined to rescue Israel and begin a new age where God will write his law on human hearts rather than tablets of stone (Jer. 31:33). In all 39 occurrences in the Old Testament, the Greek version (Septuagint) translates it as *Christos*, from which we derive the title "Christ." Prophets, priests and kings were all anointed with oil when commissioned to their respective office. Jesus the Messiah was anointed by the Holy Spirit at the baptism of John and fulfills all three offices.

Natures (Q. 52) – (referring to the person of Christ) the two unique, yet indivisible essences of who he is. In one person, Christ has two natures - that is, the divine essence and the human essence, with all of the properties of each. His divine nature can be seen in his holiness, power, preexistence, etc. His human nature can be seen in being born, eating, growing, experiencing pain, etc. These two natures exist fully and perfectly in the person of Christ.

New Jerusalem (Q. 152) - the final, eternal city that comes down out of heaven to rest upon a new earth at the end of time (Rev. 21-22:5; Isa. 65:17; 2 Peter 3:12-13). This is the marriage of heaven and earth, the new abode of God where his presence and power will dwell eternally, and his children will finally and fully behold God the Father and his Son *face to face* (Rev. 22:3-4; Matt. 5:8; 2 Cor. 4:6).

Offices (Q. 76) - the term used to describe the various aspects of Christ's relationship with his people in his work of redemption. In all things, Christ is the "one mediator between God and men" (1 Tim. 2:5), but as our mediator, he represents us before God in three different ways: as Prophet, Priest and King. These offices correspond to the three special roles God established for the nation of Israel which Jesus fulfills perfectly.

Original Sin (Q. 40) - the sin of Adam in the Garden of Eden against God's holy will that brought sin into the entire human race.

Paradise (Q. 150) - refers, in this catechism, to either the New Jerusalem or the garden of Eden, where the Tree of Life is found (Gen. 2:9; Rev. 22:2).

Pentecost (Q. 89) - the Greek term for the Old Testament "Feast of Weeks" (Lev. 23:15-22), which occurred seven weeks (50 days) after Passover and was a celebration of the first crop (or first fruits) of God's bounty in the spring harvest. For Christians, the day of Pentecost celebrates the day when Jesus sent the promised Holy Spirit to indwell and empower his disciples, 50 days after his resurrection. In one sense, the Holy Spirit is sent as the first harvest with the promise of more to come; in another, he gathers the first harvest of his church as Peter preached and 3,000 were saved (Acts 2:41).

Promises of Christ (Q. 95) - all the promises given by God in Holy Scripture, culminated and fulfilled in union with Christ alone (2 Cor. 1:20; Rom. 10:4). See "Union with Christ."

Redemption (Q. 100) - the purchasing of freedom by paying a ransom. Salvation may be free for us, but it was not free to purchase; it came at a steep price: the innocent blood of the sinless Son of God (Matt. 20:28; 1 Tim. 2:6; Eph. 1:7; Heb. 9:12; Gal. 3:13; 4:5). Titus 2:14 tells us that believers are redeemed *from* something (sin/lawlessness; also the wrath of God in Rom. 5:9), and redeemed *for* someone (to be his own possession), to be "zealous for good works." We are thus set free from the guilt, shame and power of sin along with its eternal consequences because "if the Son sets you free, you will be free indeed" (John 8:36). Once set free, his chosen instruments are expected to keep on living and walking in his freedom and not return again to the slavery of sin (1 Cor. 6:19-20; Gal. 5:1). However, while all believers are set immediately and spiritually free from the *power* of sin (Rom. 6, 8), they must still await a future day of redemption when they will be set free from the *presence* and effects of sin (Eph. 4:30; Luke 21:28), and God "'will wipe away every tear from their eyes, and death shall be no more, ... for the former things have passed away'" (Rev. 21:4; see also Rom. 8:20-23; Isa. 51:11).

Regeneration (Q. 70) - literally meaning "new birth," referring to the work of the Holy Spirit in the life of an unbeliever to transform his heart completely (Titus 3:5). Jesus describes this work in John 3:3 by saying, "Truly, truly, I say to you, unless one is born again he cannot see the kingdom of God," and he, too, attributes this work to the Holy Spirit (John 3:5, 8). The new birth is the sovereign act of God through which a person who is dead in their sins is made alive in Christ (Eph. 2:5).

Repentance (Q. 63) - both a change of mind about Jesus as Lord and Savior and a change of mind about the sin that keeps us from him. True repentance, like true, saving faith, always results in action (Luke 3:8-14; Acts 3:19; 2 Cor. 5:17; Gal. 5:19-23). Also like faith and all of salvation (Eph. 2:8-10), repentance is a free gift of God's grace (John 6:44; Acts 5:31; 11:18). While one may disown sin when he comes to Christ, there is a need for daily dying to self and daily living to Christ that occurs until his return.

Sanctification (Q. 94) - set apart by the Lord and consecrated unto the Lord. Sanctification involves both *positional, progressive* and *perfect* sanctification (see pg. 47 and Qs. 95-96). Progressive sanctification is what the catechism questions are especially aimed at addressing.

Seals (Q. 100) - a work of the Holy Spirit by which he claims a new believer as his own for all eternity. The image is that of a king pressing his signet ring into the wax seal on an important document. Everyone knows not to open it and to keep it protected because the seal of the King is present.

Second Coming (Q. 139) - the time in the future when God the Father gives the command for Jesus Christ to return to the earth to resurrect believers and the wicked and establish his eternal kingdom in a new heaven and new earth. (Matt. 24:36, Acts 1:11, Rev. 21-22).

Sinful Flesh (Q. 98) - refers to the natural evil/sinful/unholy inclinations of human nature as passed on throughout humanity since the original sin of Adam (Gen. 6:5; Jer. 17:9; Matt. 15:19; 1 Cor. 2:14). This appears especially connected to this fallen physical body (Rom. 6:6; 7:24) from which our spirit groans as we wait for the redemption of our bodies at the resurrection (Rom. 8:23). Until then, fleshly inclinations and Spirit-filled desires war against each other within our souls (Gal. 5:17). However, we are nonetheless called to walk in the Spirit, not the flesh (Gal. 5:16; Rom. 8:1-11), which is possible because we are no longer slaves to sin (Rom. 6).

Spirit (Q. 140) - the immaterial part of humanity that animates life in the physical body, survives death in an intermediate state and rises within a new body on the day of the Lord. There is debate about whether there is a distinction between "soul," and "spirit" (e.g., Heb. 4:12), making humanity material (body) with two parts that are immaterial (i.e., soul, spirit), thus a trichotomy. Others rightly point out that the terms are interchangeable (so Luke 1:46-47 compared to John 13:21 compared to Rev. 6:9), making humanity a dichotomy (material and immaterial; Matt. 10:28; Rom. 12:1-2; 2:28-29; 1 Cor. 7:34; 5:5; James 2:26; 2 Cor. 7:1; 4:16;). (See Wayne Grudem's *Systematic Theology*, chapter 23.)

Spiritual Gifts (Q. 101) - special talents, desires or interests given uniquely to Christians by God's grace (e.g., Rom. 12:3-8; 1 Cor. 12; 14) for the encouragement, edification and growth of the saints. While given at the moment of spiritual surrender to Jesus, these gifts must be nurtured and cultivated for the rest of our lives (2 Tim. 1:6). Spiritual gifts may be discovered through trial and error, wise counsel or the laying on of hands by elders (1 Tim. 4:14). Each believer in Christ is given a minimum of one, and often is given more than one. Paul admonishes the Corinthians twice to "earnestly desire" the greater gifts (1 Cor. 12:31; 14:1; i.e., the ones that build others up). However, all Christians are called to share the gospel, to love one another and to be hospitable, whether they have those gifts or not.

Triune (Q. 157) - a way to describe the truth that there is only one God, who exists eternally in three distinct persons: Father,

Son and Holy Spirit. Each person of the Trinity is fully divine, and yet distinct from the other two.

Unchanging (Q. 11) - an incommunicable attribute of God by which he is unchanging in his nature and essence (Ps. 33:11; Isa. 46:8-11; James 1:17).

Union with Christ (Q. 119) - (in the context of baptism) refers to a believer symbolically identifying with Jesus' death and burial in the tomb by going under the water, and his resurrection when brought out. On a deeper level, union with Christ is the source of all spiritual blessings from beginning to end. This includes salvation, from which flows predestination (Eph. 1:4), justification (Rom. 8:1), sanctification (1 Cor. 1:30) and glorification (1 Cor. 15:22). Union with Christ is not just another aspect of salvation, it is both the center hub from which all the spokes of redemption branch out and the larger wheel that holds them all together. The two aspects of this union are often described as our *objective union* and our *subjective union*. The objective union emphasizes Christ's work and Christ's righteousness as something outside and alien to us. We are *in Christ* from eternity past, not because of anything we have done, but by God's free grace decision (Eph. 1:4; Rom. 9:16). The subjective union emphasizes that Christ becomes *ours* when we believe and the Holy Spirit is poured into our hearts. In this sense, Scripture speaks of *Christ in us* (Gal. 2:20; Col. 1:27; Rom. 8:10). What God has joined together therefore, let not man, nor angel, nor demon nor tumultuous life circumstances separate (Rom. 8:39). (See Anthony Hoekema's *Saved by Grace,* chapter 4.)

Will (Q. 33) - God is complex, and therefore functions with different wills. Typically, theologians speak of his *sovereign will* that he alone knows, his *preceptive will* revealed in the Bible via commands and principles and "precepts," and his *permissive will* by which he allows his creation to follow their desires, even if it leads away from him. In Question 33, "ignoring his will" refers to his preceptive will. In this sense, God's preceptive will and his moral law are really synonyms, but for our purposes we use "ignoring his will" to refer to his revealed will in the Bible and "disobeying his law" to refer to rebelling against his moral law written on the heart.

Yahweh (Q. 3) - the personal name of God given to Moses at the burning bush (Ex. 3:13-14). In Hebrew, only four letters are present: Y-H-W-H, meaning "I am." It is the most frequently used name of God, occurring nearly 7,000 times in the Old Testament (almost 700 times in the Psalms alone).

Topical Index

All number references indicate associated questions and/or answers.

Adam/Eve 22-26, 29-31, 34-40
Attributes of God 7, 9-15
Baptism 117-119, 123
Bible/Scripture 43-44, 102-110
God 1-21, 23-30, 32-33, 35-37, 43-50, 55, 62, 72, 80-84, 129-130, 134, 159
Church/Community 110-117, 124-126, 131
Conditional Immortality 67, 145
Covenant 80-81, 84-85
Creation 16-29, 37
Death 39, 56, 141-142, 155
Faith 72, 74, 108, 118
Fruit of the Spirit 92-93
Glory/Glorify 18, 133-134, 156
Gospel 63, 66-68
Holy Spirit 2, 5, 51, 71, 88-95, 100-102, 104, 158
Hope 137, 141
Idolatry 32-33

Immortality 24, 28, 67, 145
Intermediate State 142
Jesus Christ 4, 50-60, 63, 66, 69, 73-88, 90, 97, 99, 111, 113, 116-117, 123, 129, 131, 138-140, 146, 149, 159
Joy 18, 93, 153, 157-158
Judgment 36, 39, 47, 49, 55, 139, 143-144, 159
Kingdom 132-133, 135, 148, 153
Law 33, 43-46, 74, 81-83, 85-87
Lord's Supper/Communion 117, 120-123
Messiah 4, 73, 76, 82
New Heavens/New Earth 1, 137, 146-159
Ordinances 117-119, 120-123
Original Sin 40-41, 53
Peace 93, 153, 155-156, 158
Prayer 102, 124, 127, 129-132
Repentance 63-64, 69, 123
Resurrection 137-146
Righteous/Righteousness 61, 138, 145, 153-154, 158
Rule/Reign 25, 33, 79, 135, 149, 151-152
Sacraments 117-119, 120-123
Salvation 49-72, 100
Sanctification 93-100
Savior 4, 49-72, 91, 113, 123
Second Coming 66, 139
Sin 30-49, 53, 55, 63-65, 98
Sinful Nature 41-42, 95-96
Social Justice 135
Suffering 39, 137, 141
Trinity 2-6

Advent Christian Declaration of Principles

1. We believe that the Bible is the inspired Word of God, being in its entirety a revelation given to man under divine inspiration and providence; that its historic statements are correct, and that it is the only divine and infallible standard of faith and practice.
2. We believe, as revealed in the Bible:
    a. In one God, our Father, eternal, and infinite in his wisdom, love and power, the Creator of all things, "in whom we live, and move, and have our being."
    b. And in Jesus Christ, our Lord, the only begotten Son of God, conceived of the Holy Spirit, born of the Virgin Mary; who came into our world to seek and to save that which was lost; who died for our sins; who was raised bodily from the dead for our justification; who ascended in heaven as our High Priest and Mediator, and who will come again in the end of

this age, to judge the living and the dead, and to reign forever and ever.

    c. And in the Holy Spirit, the Comforter, sent from God to convince the world of sin, of righteousness and of judgment, whereby we are sanctified and sealed unto the day of redemption.

3. We believe that man was created for immortality, but that through sin he forfeited his divine birthright; that because of sin, death entered into the world, and passed upon all men; and that only through faith in Jesus Christ, the divinely ordained Life-giver, can men become "partakers of the divine nature," and live forever.

4. We believe that death is a condition of unconsciousness to all persons, righteous and wicked; a condition which will remain unchanged until the resurrection at Christ's Second Coming, at which time the righteous will receive everlasting life while the wicked will be "punished with everlasting destruction;" suffering complete extinction of being.

5. We believe that salvation is free to all those who, in this life and in this age, accept it on the conditions imposed, which conditions are simple and inflexible, namely, turning from sin, repentance toward God, faith in the Lord Jesus Christ, and a life of consecration to the service of God; thus excluding all hope of a future probation, or of universal salvation.

Advent Christian Declaration Of Principles

6. We believe that Jesus Christ, according to his promise, will come again to this earth, even "in like manner" as he went into heaven – personally, visibly and gloriously – to reign here forever; and that this coming is the hope of the church, inasmuch as upon that coming depend the resurrection and reward of the righteous, the abolition of sin and its consequences, and the renewal of the earth – now marred by sin – to become the eternal home of the redeemed, after which event the earth will be forever free from sin and death.

7. We believe that Bible prophecy has indicated the approximate time of Christ's return; and comparing its testimony with the signs of our times, we are confident the he is near, "even at the doors," and we believe that the great duty of the hour is the proclamation of this soon-coming redemption, the defense of Bible authority, inspiration and truth, and the salvation of lost men.

8. We believe the church of Christ is an institution of divine origin, which includes all true Christians, of whatever name; but that local church organizations should be independent of outside control, congregational in government, and subject to no dictation of priest, bishop or pope – although true fellowship and unity of action should exist between all such organizations.

9. We believe that the only ordinances of the church of Christ are Baptism and the Lord's Supper; immersion being the only true baptism.

10. We believe that the first day of the week, as the day set apart by the early church in commemoration of Christ's resurrection, should be observed as the Christian Sabbath, and used as a day of rest and religious worship.
11. We believe that war is contrary to the spirit and teachings of our Lord and Master, Jesus Christ; that it is contrary to the spirit of true brotherhood; and that our influence should be used against it. We believe the Bible also teaches that properly constituted government is ordained of God and is a divine instrument for man's welfare and protection. When an Advent Christian decides on the basis of Scripture and conscience, either to bear arms or to submit to penalties imposed for his refusal to do so, local Advent Christian congregations should extend continued fellowship and nurture.

Advent Christian Statement of Faith

We believe the Bible to be the inspired, the only infallible, authoritative Word of God.

We believe that there is one God, eternally existent in three persons: Father, Son and Holy Spirit.

We believe in the deity of our Lord Jesus Christ, in His virgin birth, in His sinless life, in His miracles, in His vicarious and atoning death through His shed blood, in His bodily resurrection, in His ascension to the right hand of the Father, and in His personal return in power and glory.

We believe that for the salvation of lost and sinful people, regeneration by the Holy Spirit is absolutely essential.

We believe in the present ministry of the Holy Spirit by whose indwelling the Christian is enabled to live a godly life.

We believe in the resurrection of both the saved and the lost; they that are saved unto the resurrection of life and they that are lost unto the resurrection of damnation.

We believe in the spiritual unity of believers in our Lord Jesus Christ.

CPSIA information can be obtained
at www.ICGtesting.com
Printed in the USA
BVHW041118240219
541026BV00017B/557/P